Other Books by Rebekah Simon-Peter

Green Church
Reduce, Reuse, Recycle, Rejoice!

Green Church
Reduce, Reuse, Recycle, Rejoice! Leader Guide
With Pamela Dilmore

7 Simple Steps to Green Your Church

The Jew Named Jesus
Discover the Man and His Message

Dream Like Jesus
Deepen Your Faith and Bring the Impossible to Life

D1413280

EMBRACING THE NEXT NORMAL

forging
a new path

moving the church forward
in a post-pandemic world

REBEKAH SIMON-PETER

Market
Square
BOOKS

forging
a new path
moving the church forward
in a post-pandemic world

by Rebekah Simon-Peter

©2022 Rebekah Simon-Peter

books@marketsquarebooks.com
141 N. Martinwood Dr., Knoxville TN 37923

ISBN: 978-1-950899-59-3

Printed and Bound in the United States of America

Cover Illustration & Book Design
©2022 Market Square Publishing, LLC

Editor: Sheri Carder Hood
Post Production Editor: Ken Rochelle

Scripture quotations used with permission from:

CEB
Scripture quotations from the COMMON ENGLISH BIBLE. © Copyright 2011 COMMON
ENGLISH BIBLE. All rights reserved. Used by permission. (www.CommonEnglishBible.com).

ESV
The Holy Bible: English Standard Version
Scripture quotations marked "ESV" are taken from The Holy Bible: English Standard Version,
copyright © 2001, Wheaton: Good News Publishers. Used by permission. All rights reserved.

MSG
Scripture quotations marked MSG are taken from THE MESSAGE,
copyright © 1993, 2002, 2018 by Eugene H. Peterson. Used by permission of NavPress,
represented by Tyndale House Publishers. All rights reserved.

NRSV
New Revised Standard Version Bible, copyright © 1989 National Council
of the Churches of Christ in the United States of America.
Used by permission. All rights reserved worldwide.

NIV
Scriptures marked NIV are taken from the NEW INTERNATIONAL VERSION (NIV):
Scripture taken from THE HOLY BIBLE, NEW INTERNATIONAL VERSION ®.
Copyright ©1973, 1978, 1984, 2011 by Biblica, Inc.™. Used by permission of Zondervan.

Table of Contents

Introduction

The prophet Ezekiel surveyed a valley of dry bones and was asked by the Lord, "Son of man, can these bones live?" Ezekiel answered, "Sovereign LORD, you alone know." Ezekiel 37:3 (NIV). Ezekiel's vision hinted at the dry lifelessness of a people in exile, centuries ago. Now, in the twenty-first century, his question echoes through time in a new way for people of faith displaced by the pandemic. Can these churches live? For people who care about faith-based communities, the Gospel of Jesus Christ, and the Kin(g)dom of God, this question is critical. When the pandemic broke out, it badly disrupted church life, already hindered by declining membership, forcing pastors and church members alike to ask once more, "Can these churches live?"

In my work with churches and church leaders across the nation, I've had a unique opportunity to think about possible answers to this question. The three-year process I founded and developed called Creating a Culture of Renewal® teaches churches and their leaders how to interrupt decline, accelerate vitality, and redirect

1

congregations to *Dream Like Jesus*® once again. Each year my team of faculty and I lead more than 150 church leaders to engage in this rigorous process of rethinking leadership and congregational development. Throughout the three-year program, participants expand their congregational intelligence, leadership smarts, and culture-shifting abilities. In Creating a Culture of Renewal®, our approach to renewal begins not from wresting hope out of circumstantial doom and gloom, but from promises borne of deep reliance and trust in Jesus' own faith. It's clear to us that Jesus trusted in the wisdom and faithfulness of God, in the miraculous, and in the power of God's divine revelation. Tapping into this faith allows us to forge a new path.

To better understand and respond to the impacts of the pandemic, I draw upon the approach we take in Creating a Culture of Renewal® for one simple reason: this is the approach that Jesus took. He no more let wind and waves stop him than we should let pandemics stop us. That doesn't mean we don't grieve the millions of lives lost around the globe; we do. Nor does it mean that we don't take injustice and inequities seriously; we do. During the first year of the pandemic, people's health and well-being were obviously threatened; injustice and inequity were keenly revealed. However, these ongoing vulnerabilities create greater urgency for the church to find new footing even under the most difficult circumstances. I believe we must bring an empowered sense of what is possible to the conversation about the future of the church.

To do so, I've arranged this book according to the questions that people in churches all across the country are asking. After listening to people's greatest concerns, I've heard them ask three persistent questions: When do things go back to normal? How do we get people (back) to church? How do we do more with less?

To find answers to these questions, I looked at pandemics past to see how medieval Christians dealt with these same issues. Their answers were surprising. In fact, they are the kind of answers that lead me to believe that this is the perfect time for us to envision and forge a new path forward with God. In this book, I'm going to share with you what I believe we can learn from our past about how to reshape our future. I'll give you a heads up. Reshaping our future won't come from superficial or technical changes, but from profound changes in the way we live out being the church. To explain, illustrate, and support my ideas, I'll also reveal firsthand perspectives from Creating a Culture of Renewal® participants whose challenges and successes in creating congregational renewal throughout the pandemic will be insightful for you.

Even as the ancient question, "Can these bones live?" resonates across the centuries, so too does Scripture's answer: "This is what the Sovereign LORD says to these bones, 'I will make breath enter you and you will come to life'" Ezekiel 37:5 (NIV). Vivified by God's Spirit, may this book breathe new life into pandemic-weary churches and leaders so that we too come to life, ready to embrace the next normal.

CHAPTER ONE

The Day the World Changed . . . Again

I remember exactly where I was twenty-one years
ago when I heard that the World Trade Center had
been attacked on September 11, 2001. I was about to
walk into the weekly Clergy Association breakfast
meeting at the Square Shooters restaurant in downtown
Rawlins, Wyoming, where I served as a pastor. Loretta,
the mother of one of my youth, was walking out of the
restaurant as I was walking in. "Have you heard? The
Twin Towers in New York City have been attacked."

What? My mind went blank. I couldn't comprehend
what she was saying. I thought maybe she was joking,
but I couldn't figure out why. It wasn't until much later
in the day, as the news filtered in, that the pieces began
to come together. A day like 9/11 is hard to forget; it will
forever be imprinted in my mind. I knew, somehow, that
the world had changed forever. After that day, life didn't
go back to normal. Before 9/11, for instance, air travel
was relatively carefree. Post-9/11, air travel worldwide
became an obstacle course. Arrive two hours early,
expect long lines at security, take your shoes off, ease

your laptop out of your bag, and don't forget that no more than three ounces of a liquid are permitted. Forget about taking a bottle of water or a cup of coffee through security. Ain't gonna happen.

Although we in the United States couldn't have known it back then, September 11, 2001, became a day that set the stage for where we found ourselves during the coronavirus pandemic. Just after 9/11, citizens came together in solidarity and patriotism. Church attendance grew, and expressions of faith rose. The majority of Americans were willing to make personal changes to prevent further terror attacks. But over the next two decades, our society began to segment and polarize. Some took a very negative view of Muslims, saying they were not part of mainstream U.S. society. As anti-Muslim sentiment grew, so did political polarization. Divisiveness and disinformation also seeped into our everyday lives, made more viral and vicious through burgeoning social media, podcasts, and media outlets.

In the same way that I remember where I was when I got the news of 9/11, I also remember where I was when I first heard about the coronavirus erupting in Wuhan, the capital city of the Hubei province in China. That day, the world changed again. But I didn't know it then. On that day, I was on a plane headed home from a first-ever, carefree Hawaiian vacation. As we awaited takeoff, I checked my Facebook feed and saw a story about a virus outbreak restricting movement and travel. I remember thinking, "Geez, those poor people in China," before moving on to the next story. At the time, I could never have envisioned that restricted movement and travel would become the norm for all of us and that this would be my last flight ANYWHERE for a very long time.

How Our Lives Have Changed

A few weeks later, March 12, 2020, rolled around – the day the World Health Organization declared the coronavirus a global pandemic. On that same day, Dr. Anthony Fauci, Director of the National Institutes of Allergy and Infectious Diseases, testified before Congress that COVID-19 was ten times more deadly than the seasonal flu. A cascade of surprising, sometimes shocking, events occurred. Then-President Trump added a 30-day suspension of travel from continental Europe to the U.S. to a ban already in place between the U.S. and China; the ban ultimately extended another twenty months for China and another nineteen months for Europe. The NBA suspended its season, and spectators were banned from March Madness. Tom and Rita Hanks announced they had contracted the coronavirus, and stocks plunged. It was a monumental day.

At the time, my state of Wyoming had no cases of coronavirus and no deaths. Even so, within a week or two, the first signs went up in buildings around the town where I live. "Closed for three weeks. Will reopen." Favorite restaurants, shops, and even churches shuttered their doors and windows. Three weeks seemed like a very long time. Those three weeks came and went, but restaurants, shops, and churches remained locked tight. Three weeks turned into four weeks, which then turned into five. Weeks stretched into months.

In the meantime, pastors began live-streaming worship. YouTube channels and Facebook channels lit up. No longer flying around the country to work with church leaders – or even to visit my aging parents – I spent a lot of time at home, inside. But flying isn't the only thing that went away. Hugs, handshakes, and most physical contact with others evaporated. My husband, Jerry, was the only person I got physically close to. Thank goodness for my dog, Beau, who I could still hug.

When I went out, I socially distanced. One day I noticed that even when I drove, I kept my car farther away from other cars. This was a very different world: small, restricted, cautious. Going to the grocery store was an adventure in staying away from other people and trying to find what my family needed from the picked-over shelves. I wondered if we would ever truly leave our homes again. It felt surreal.

While many of us felt a time of deep spiritual need, church members did not know how and when to show up to church. So used to the strength and comfort of fellowship we found in physical gatherings (not to mention sharing food), we mourned the loss of congregating. In the meantime, the cadence of pastors' lives changed dramatically. Although many churches gathered online, more work than ever went into creating and producing worship services. Pastors live-streamed worship from empty sanctuaries, living rooms, and makeshift sound studios – and they did it without visual or verbal feedback. Worship, which relies on interactive energies, became more like a lonely radio broadcast, sometimes conducted over one smartphone.

Yet, in the midst of this constraint, unprecedented creativity borne under pressure was set free. Church, traditionally confined to the insides of buildings, moved online and even outside. With online worship taking hold in about 50 percent of congregations nationwide, the previously homebound could now participate in worship. People from other towns, cities, states, regions, and countries could easily drop in on locally produced worship experiences. Overnight, the reach of the Gospel both contracted and expanded – an astonishing experience!

Even as people gathered in brand new ways, unbound by physical proximity or shared time zones, streets and highways were quiet and hauntingly empty. At 8 p.m. every night, shouts of support went up in neighborhoods across the country for front-line workers. The sense of unity was palpable.

Then, a series of deaths of Black citizens at the hands

of police officers began to pepper the news. Breonna Taylor and George Floyd became household names. People of all races and ethnicities poured into the streets to march for Black Lives Matter.

In my small Wyoming city, thousands of people came together, masks on, led by a local pastor, to signal our grief, outrage, and solidarity with all who marched across our country. As we walked peacefully through downtown Casper on our way to the police department – where we were greeted with courtesy and understanding – we passed dozens of self-appointed White nationalist vigilantes stationed on the street corners with AK-47s slung around their necks. While no altercations occurred in our city, riots broke out in other locations around the country, fires burned, and clashes between police, protesters, and counter-protesters gained national and international headlines.

When our own U.S. president called COVID-19 the "China virus," some began targeting Asians and Asian Americans as the source of the coronavirus. One South Korean colleague of mine reported that local neighborhood kids taunted his two young children and his wife for starting the coronavirus. Visiting the parents of these children led to an opening in their relationship and to new dialogue within their community. But a negative focus on Asians continued in this country. One year after the initial pandemic shutdowns, a White male gunman killed eight people at Atlanta-area massage parlors. Six of the eight people killed were women of Asian descent. Many Asian women feared for their lives – traumatized, hunkered down, and afraid to leave their homes – as news videos showed random beatings of innocent Asian Americans simply walking down the street. A United Methodist pastor, the Rev. Naomi Rogers was the first Asian female to be ordained in Arkansas. No stranger to overcoming fear, she told us of the paralyzing fear she endured at the time of the killings, and how hard she had to work for many months afterward, just to show her face in public.

Hunger, homelessness, and joblessness also dominated the news. Long lines of cars snaked around city blocks, people waiting their turn to accept a bag of food from food banks and distribution centers. In many locations, there wasn't enough to go around.

At the same time the coronavirus was impacting the world, a U.S. presidential race was underway. Politics became nastier than ever during the 2020 presidential election. Mail-in ballots flooded voting precincts and disturbed previously held expectations about how and when results would be tallied. As the nation waited for hours, then days, for definitive results, upset roiled the country when it became clear that presidential powers would transfer from Donald Trump to Joe Biden. Yet, this was anything but a peaceful transfer of power. On January 6, 2021, a violent attack on the U.S. Capitol by followers of the former president created fear and uncertainty for many, especially for Black and Jewish Americans as the insurrection was accompanied by Confederate flags and swastikas. Even as Kamala Harris, the first female and biracial vice president, took her place in history, a protracted denial of the fair 2020 election results began – and continues today – as a disturbing undercurrent in American life, undermining democracy and a sense of peace and security.

When stores and restaurants began to open up in 2021, even with masks, life started to feel more normal again. Vaccines were released for all adults and then for children six and older. Many months after the start of the pandemic, I finally put my mask away and started to feel safe again. Then, the delta variant quickly made the rounds, ratcheting up infections and deaths, followed by the omicron variant.

Here we are, more than two years later, still grasping the enormity of this COVID-19 pandemic. My own family lost several members. Former parishioners, friends, and colleagues have succumbed to the virus. ICUs have operated at capacity, and sometimes beyond, in waves across the country and around the world. In the early days, it wasn't clear if vaccines could ever be developed or how long they might take to move through the stages of development. Then, some people began to protest masks and vaccines, crying out for "medical freedom." This mask and vaccine hesitancy extended the infectious rate. At the same time, anti-viral medications were made available that could diminish the symptoms and severity of COVID-19.

Since the COVID-19 pandemic began, the world has changed in many ways. Not just the six million people worldwide who have died and left family and friends to mourn. Or the one million people in the U.S. who have succumbed to it, leaving their family and friends in grief. Or the long haulers who deal with ongoing symptoms for who knows how long. We as a society have changed; the church has changed.

How the Church Has Changed

Churches and other houses of worship have been profoundly affected by the pandemic. Most often, churches and other houses of worship where people gather in the tens, hundreds, and thousands – considered essential for so many of us – were deemed "nonessential services." Public gatherings, when allowed, were limited to ten people. Ironically, even as religious gatherings were deemed nonessential, liquor stores garnered the opposite designation and were allowed to remain open for business.

The decision to categorize churches as nonessential deeply impacted already declining congregational vitality. In this decision, public health mandates and spiritual traditions collided.[1] Stay-at-home orders took effect in many places. The act of congregating became almost impossible. Mask mandates added to the sense of social isolation. Congregations experienced the deaths of both members and pastors, while having limited ability to grieve within their community or engage in familiar rites and rituals with family and friends for support.

Public opinion varied on the wisdom of shuttering houses of worship. While some people looked at the closed doors of church buildings as an act of self-sacrifice undertaken for the common good, others interpreted the mandated closings as an attack on religious freedom. They saw it as a curtailment of spiritual succor precisely when when it was most needed. Churches that remained open provided spiritual sustenance while undermining public health since they sometimes became "super-spreader" events.

Some Republican and Democratic governors granted exemptions to churches in their states so they could continue to meet, while other Republican and Democratic governors declared churches in their states to be nonessential. Because of this divergent approach toward public gatherings oriented around spiritual needs, individual congregations themselves were often conflicted, especially congregations whose conduct was governed by denominational authorities that were geographically removed.

Some church members insisted that they should be allowed to meet. Or alternatively, they definitely shouldn't meet; it's not safe. Others insisted on masks and were okay with not singing since the virus traveled on airborne particles. Others, tired of constraints and mourning the loss of familiar ways, complained about or refused to wear masks. Those conflicts were a natural expression of people who felt powerless, frustrated, afraid, and impacted by situations beyond their control. But underlying, unresolved conflicts – often split along partisan lines – made it tough for churches to move forward in unity.

In addition to the ongoing political divides that have caused hard feelings and impacted churches dramatically, the whole experience of people dying and loved ones not being able to grieve in the usual ways, mourn communally, or mark a person's passing through public, face-to-face funerals and memorials have slowed people's ability to rebound. We have been weighed down by unprocessed grief.[2]

CHAPTER TWO

Three Persistent Questions

When Do Things Go Back to Normal?

Given the events of 2020, 2021, and 2022 that have dramatically impacted and changed the landscape in which churches operate, it's important to address three persistent questions I hear people asking. The first question on most people's minds has been, "When do things go back to normal?"

In the church, normal means greeting each other with hugs and handshakes and singing together in worship. Normal means taking Holy Communion in the company of others. It means sharing air with favorite people. It means returning to live, in-person worship with the same people we were used to seeing before, while also welcoming new folks. Normal means getting back to the ministries we used to offer, and traveling freely without fear. Normal means recovering from the shutdowns, coming back together, and getting past the pandemic. And maybe normal now means including the online options we have come to employ.

So when *do* things go back to normal?

Many churches have long journeyed back to the familiar. Others are quickly making up for lost time. They are serving Holy Communion at the altar rail, followed by maskless mingling at coffee hour and a brisk schedule of in-person meetings. I'm all for in-person worship and relaxing in the company of others. After all, we are social creatures. Being together like "before" nourishes the heart and is good for the soul. There's just one problem with going back to the familiar, but most people don't want to hear this. "Normal" doesn't exist anymore. There's no going back to 2019.

And, even if churches could go back to normal, the rest of the world wouldn't be joining us. That's because lives have changed. People have picked up new habits and established new patterns. Life, in general, is not magically going back to a time before COVID-19.

Before the pandemic, the congregation I attended hosted two Sunday services. My favorite service took place at 8:30 a.m. with lively music that attracted both younger families and singles, including Bea, whose strong step, easy smile, and gorgeous white head of hair belied the fact that she was in her ninth decade of life. Bea attracted friends wherever she went; she and her pals filled a whole pew. She attracted me too; I sat right in front of "her" row. Bea's presence and energy contributed to the vibe of the service. In addition to the lively worship at 8:30 a.m., worshipers gathered at 11 a.m. for a more traditional service.

During the pandemic, when the doors of the church closed, my Sunday schedule changed dramatically. My parents started a weekly family Zoom meeting from 9 to 10 a.m. My mother's advanced ALS meant she could no longer talk, walk, move, or even eat. She was now on a feeding tube. Seeing all of us during our weekly Sunday morning Zoom meetings lifted her spirits, as well as ours. Since phone conversations no longer worked with mom, meeting online created easier access for communication. My siblings, our partners and spouses, kids, nieces, nephews, aunts, and uncles attended. Family members sprawled out over three U.S. time zones and a few European ones as well have made sure to call in. On more than one occasion, my singer/songwriter nephew, Michael, joined us from Berlin, guitar in hand and keyboard at the ready. At other times, my nephew Max, fresh from his shift as a food server in the Netherlands, joined in the call, too.

As a whole, we haven't missed a single week for twenty-five months and counting. During this time, we have celebrated my parents' eighty-fourth and eighty-fifth birthdays and sixty-third and sixty-fourth anniversaries. We've absorbed cancer diagnoses, rejoiced at successful surgeries, talked about work, and shared favorite memories. Over the last two years, I've seen more of my whole family than I ever have before; something really special has developed here. I hate to miss a single family meeting.

It's not all fun and laughter, though. The conversation has sometimes turned tense, spilling over into offline texting and hard-to-have phone conversations. We have expressed diverging opinions about masks, vaccines, and the 2020 election. This is true community – with all the joys and concerns that a congregation would experience – except rawer and more connected.

When my local congregation reopened its doors and live worship resumed, I was definitely torn. Do I go back to church as I did pre-pandemic? What about my newfound relationship with my family and the sense of community we share? Life had changed since March 2020, and I had changed with it. Even me, a person who has devoted her life to religious organizations and spiritual community, feels torn about attending church now. It is not because I have lost my faith, but because I have found community in new places. My schedule and commitments have shifted.

I am not the only one who finds myself in this position. As of this writing, Barna Group, a research firm that studies faith in the US, estimates that "In-person church attendance is roughly 30 to 50 percent lower than it was before the pandemic."[3] In addition to folks like me whose lives have morphed into new expressions of community, people are staying away from church for all kinds of other reasons. Older people and those with greater health risks have cautiously stayed away from large gatherings. Others have simply gotten out of the habit of attending worship. My friends Ashley and Sage have embraced the convenience of attending online. Why go to church when church can come to you? Happy to worship in their pajamas from their living room or watch the recording at a later time, stay at home worshipers also includes young parents.

But fewer parents in worship often means fewer children too. This kind of change in worship attendance diminishes congregational richness and vitality. To be sustainable, congregations need a minimum of three to four active generations – not including the pastor and parsonage family.

Of those who have returned to in-person worship, the longing for normalcy is palpable. Besides drawing on my own experience, I interviewed church leaders across the country who are participants in Creating a Culture of Renewal® about their experience. "It's like Throwback Thursday," noted Rev. Leigh Goodrich. "In my Vermont community, there is such a yearning for normalcy that we are back to singing very old hymns. That's not helpful either. We have to find the middle ground." Rev. Clayton Payne noted that the "Throwback Thursday" effect in his Virginia congregation went back a lot farther than singing hymns from the early 1900s. Instead, it showed up as a desire to be so shut off from the outside world and its uncertainties as to be "cloistered."

The Christian practice of cloistering dates back to the Middle Ages when monasteries were shut off from daily life. The nuns and monks who lived in the monasteries carried out their religious duties without contact with the outside world. Members of the communities would live their entire lives inside the walls of a cloister, never to interact with people outside their religious community. Ironically, cloistered communities were highly susceptible to the pandemic of their time, the bubonic plague. Once the plague entered a community, it raced through the ranks and wiped out entire monasteries and convents. Hundreds of cloistered communities were decimated during the plague – a sad reminder that shutting yourself off from the world doesn't save you.[4]

Middle ground has been hard to locate in the ongoing uncertainty of living with the coronavirus and its variants. Rev. James B. Graham III, who pastors an active, medium-sized church in Oklahoma, revealed how the ambiguity impacted him. "Things changed week to week. In order to plan for meetings, I had to consult a website for outbreak information. From there, I decided if we were meeting in person or not, if the choir could sing or not, and if we could even have coffee hour." Over time, living on high alert drained James and other leaders of their usual stores of resilience. Even as fewer people attended worship, pastors found they were busier and needed more of a break from the direct pressures of ministry to bolster their self-care and rebuild their own spiritual well-being.

After hearing from church leaders and members alike, I understand the deep yearning to go back to the way things were. At the same time, here's the reality: there is no going back. There is only going forward. Once churches opened back up, for example, my home church consolidated its two worship services into one and moved the time of worship to the 10 a.m. hour. While this change is not a sign of growth – the worshiping congregation is reduced by about 50 percent – it gathers the remaining worshipers into one setting, creates a sense of togetherness, and positions the congregation to build momentum. Selfishly, on any given Sunday, it also means I can both Zoom with members of my personal family and then worship with my church family – or at least do part of both. Sadly, though, the worshiping community I returned to has changed. Beautiful Bea is gone – she passed on during the pandemic – and her row of friends has scattered as well.

More than two years out from the start of the pandemic, it's clear that our lives are different. Just because the pandemic is receding does not mean life spontaneously resets to 2019 or that people automatically resume their previous schedules and commitments. People have both more and less going on. And some of what is going on is just plain different.

The Forgotten Problem with Normal

So the old normal of 2019 no longer exists. Life has evolved along with the virus, showing up in all kinds of new variants. Today we find ourselves in brand new terrain. While you could try to go back to the same worship service, the same meetings, the same discussions and debates, if you did, you would also return to the forgotten problem with "normal," which is that the normal way of doing church had actually become a model for decline. As Rev. McKenzie Sefa, a member of the Creating a Culture of Renewal® faculty, noted, "Churches know they can't go back to 2019. What they believe, though, is that they can bring 2019 back to life in 2022. The same events are going back on the calendar, the same worship service is being brought forward, and the same worries about decreasing membership and financial struggles are approached from the same perspective."

Yet long before the pandemic erupted, churches were already worried about their health and vitality. Younger generations and their parents weren't as interested in church as previous generations. Of the children that did come, many "graduated" after receiving their Bibles in third grade or after being confirmed. Their parents weren't much different. After teaching endless Sunday school classes and leading years of youth group, burned-out parents often retired from active church life, passing the reins to the next generation. Boomers fretted about how to attract more children and their parents while resisting changing the worship service to meet those needs. The Pioneer generation worried if their congregation could stay vibrant long enough to ensure that at least someone would be there to conduct their funeral, even if the congregation didn't outlast them by long. These worries produced little fruit. Instead, even with their best efforts, caring and committed members of churches watched their congregations shrink and age. That's what "normal" looked like in 2019 before the pandemic hit.

The normal way of doing church wasn't just a series of unfortunate dynamics. Instead, it was a pattern of expectations woven into the very culture of church life. In my work with a wide range of churches and their leaders, it's clear that the values of stability, security, and conflict-avoidance shape the culture in many churches. Also woven into the culture of church life is the unspoken assumption that if you teach people about Jesus, explain the tenets of the faith, and give people opportunities to do good, then you will have successfully made disciples. Unfortunately, this process may work for creating church attenders and church members, but it doesn't necessarily produce committed disciples or followers of Jesus, let alone courageous apostles or ambassadors of Jesus.[5]

As our name suggests, in Creating a Culture of Renewal®, we are especially interested in the way things get done in a church. Our work with church leaders supports the theory that the culture of a congregation is not an "inactive ingredient" in the life of a church. Rather, it's an "active ingredient" that directly helps or hinders the movement of the Holy Spirit. When the culture of a congregation hinders the movement of the Spirit, then congregations tend to stagnate spiritually. When it facilitates the movement of the Holy Spirit, then congregations open up to the path of revitalization.

Simply resuming the "normal" way of doing things in church, in other words, some version of Sunday worship + Sunday school classes + small groups + administrative meetings won't make the needed difference now. While we can all be forgiven the intense desire for normalcy – the pandemic disoriented us in ways we could never have imagined – "normal" wasn't a sustainable model for building a robust life of faith or for growing a vital congregation before the pandemic. And it still isn't.

How Do We Get People (Back) to Church?

As my husband and I walked into the family Christmas Eve service in 2021, we were surprised to see the pews were almost empty. Thirty long, comfortably cushioned rows split by a middle aisle were available for seating. But not a single person was seated in the first fifteen rows. In fact, there weren't that many people seated in the second fifteen rows either. The balcony was bare.

I looked at the expanse of empty pews between the scattered families and the pulpit. My heart dropped. I remembered the days when it was my role as pastor to lead people in the worship of God. Sometimes a transformation occurred when the Spirit of God moved among us in such a meaningful way that separate individuals formed a cohesive worshiping congregation knit together by a palpable energy. But that was only accomplished by the presence of the Spirit, which wasn't a sure thing even with full pews. Feeling that Spirit is especially challenging with a lot of empty pews. Christmas Eve, far more than half of the pews were empty. Like a lonely cry in the wilderness, emptiness can suck the life out of worship.

My husband and I intentionally walked up to the front near the center aisle. Thankfully, a few other families joined us as the time of worship approached. However, this same situation – a wilderness of empty pews – has faced choirs, lay readers, and pastors since the shutdowns have ended. A recent study shows that more than one-third of worship services have decreased by 25 percent or more during 2019-2021. On a recent Sunday, I counted about fifty people present in a sanctuary designed to hold 300 to 400 people. While I'm not sure how many watched online, whether live or later, this was one-fourth the size of the worshiping congregation before the pandemic.

So how do we get people back to church – or even get them there for the first time? This is the second question on most people's minds because worshiping together is the heart of the church. Packed sanctuaries traditionally highlight holidays like Christmas, Easter, and Mother's

Day. These are the times when you want to feel the energy of a full gathering, see people you haven't seen in a while, and feel that the community has truly come together to worship. Empty pews are a tough reality to face, especially post-pandemic now that the world has opened up again.

We must acknowledge that "How do you get people back to church?" isn't a new question. It's one we've been asking for years. We must understand that this question begins with the assumption that what we were doing before the pandemic was sufficient.

Yet, we've already seen that we can't automatically resume life as it was at the end of 2019. Those days are over. Even so, we know that we have people out there who "belong" to our churches, people who are "one of us." We long to see them again and to worship side-by-side. So we continue to wrestle with how to re-assemble our congregations as the pandemic recedes.

We also know that many in our community still do not have a church home, and we know their lives – and ours – would be enriched if they were brought within the fold of our church family. So how do we get our friends, family, and neighbors to come to church for the first time? We know we have something powerful to offer, and we know we serve an important function. We know that God needs us and that the community needs us. And Lord knows we know that we need God. So how do we pick ourselves up post-pandemic and get people to church for the first time? This is, indeed, an urgent question.

Why Aren't People Coming Back to Church?

For all its problems, Facebook gives people the unique opportunity to drop in on conversations. Sometimes the conversations are refreshingly honest, even heartbreakingly raw. I watched with interest one such conversation. Rev. Sarah Payne, a Creating a Culture of Renewal® participant, who co-pastors a Virginia congregation with her husband, Clayton, reposted a popular meme on Facebook. The meme packed a punch: "You can't serve from your sofa. You can't have a community of faith on your sofa. You can't experience the power of a room full of believers worshiping together on your sofa. Christians aren't consumers. We are contributors. We don't watch. We engage. We give. We sacrifice. We encourage. We do life together. The church needs you. And you need the church." Sarah posted this with a note that following Jesus is not a passive activity but an active one.

The responses were fascinating. Many of Sarah's followers hit the "like" button. Others replied with "Amen!" Still, others objected mildly that online options gave full-time caregivers, travelers, and those out of the area a chance to participate from afar. At least one person noted that he still wasn't comfortable gathering in person. But the most insightful, thought-provoking responses came from other pastors. Joe Plemmons, a former pastor, wrote, "When the pandemic first started and everything shut down, we were all so quick to remind people that 'the Church is not a building.' And now, while we want to encourage people to stay engaged, we need to be careful with our wording so that we don't accidentally say, 'Actually, the Church *is* a building, and you need to go there.'" In other words, perhaps people aren't coming back to church because they realized that you really could worship God from anywhere, and you can be the church even when you're not in the building.

In response to the meme, a fellow Virginia pastor wrote, "I've seen this posted around, and it sort of rubs me the wrong way. I think the 'you should be in church on Sunday' misses the point. If the church isn't a place someone wants to be, it's probably not the place of healing and liberation we would like to think it is. Says more about our church model than the dedication of members that people aren't flocking back."[6]

The truth is that people have been leaving church for a long time. From 1995 to 2007, I pastored a series of churches, capped off by a small, friendly church in Rawlins, Wyoming. By the time I arrived in 1999 as the new pastor, it had been six months since the previous pastor left. During the time between pastors, a lineup of lay people had taken turns delivering a Sunday message to the congregation. The first time I stepped into the pulpit was a hot, dry August Sunday; the pews were filled. Even though worship attendance traditionally dipped in the summer, the pews remained packed for quite a few Sundays thereafter as people came to check out the new "lady" pastor.

I was the first female pastor appointed to this town of 10,000, including the prison population. The bottom line is that all kinds of people came to church during the early days of my ministry there, including many who were "coming back" to church for the first time in a long time. Predictably, some of these returnees approved of me while others disapproved. Thankfully, those who approved of me stayed, but those who tended in the other direction eventually left. My point is that people come to church, stay or leave church for a variety of reasons. This same church had been wondering how to get people "back" to church long before I got there. The truth is you wouldn't have to figure out how to get people "back" to church if they'd never left in the first place.

According to many studies, religious affiliation has waned in the decades since the Third Great Awakening of the 1950s. Church attendance has dropped year by year since 1960, with the most dramatic declines in the last ten years. While church attendance regularly fluctuates based on societal changes, studies indicate that beginning in 2000, the decline was twice as great as it was between 1960 and 1970,[7] marking this period as the Great Decline.

Research shows the top four reasons people leave church are as follows:

- A change in life situation
- The church changes for the better
- The church changes for the worse
- Growth of the spiritual but not religious movement

A Change in Life Situation

One primary reason people leave church is that their life situation has changed. They move out of town, divorce, encounter health problems, or sadly die. These changes in circumstance are part of the ebb and flow of life.

Less dramatic but equally as important is that people reach a significant milestone in life and feel that church is now part of their past instead of their future. For instance, when teens graduate from confirmation class, they may also effectively decide to "graduate" from church. We have found this especially true when these young people have little experience worshiping with adults, as is often the case in congregations where Sunday school classes take place during the worship service. When children and young people do not grow up attending worship services, once they are done with the Christian education program, they often decide they're "done" with church. Why? Because the church has not introduced or integrated them into an adult worship experience. In churches where children do attend worship, church is all too often a passive experience, one where they simply sit and listen. Yes, they may join in the singing and the responsive readings, even recite the Lord's Prayer. However, they aren't invited to help create the worship experience. They are told to live by the adage that children are to be seen and not heard. It's no wonder that when it comes time for them to make their own decision about church, they graduate and leave. These young people view the church as a part of their past, not their future.

The Church Changes for the Better

Secondly, even when a church is headed in the right direction and making positive, needed changes, there's no guarantee that everyone will be happy. As churches change locations, make significant staffing changes, adjust the time of worship, stop old programs, start new ones, or announce a new initiative or vision, not everyone wants to be part of the change.

There will always be people, who in the face of change, find they either aren't that committed to the congregation, or they simply prefer things the way they were. These may be people who come to church exactly because they liked the way things were. They aren't looking for a change. So even changes for the better can mean you will lose some people.

For example, in one congregation I know, the church finally secured a skilled, permanent pastor who could bring continuity to the congregation. As part of helping the church get grounded, she brought the congregation up to speed on some current theological discussions that previous leaders had sidestepped. This was a change for the better. But, in engaging the congregation, a number of long-time church members, finally aware of what the larger denomination was dealing with, decided to leave.

The Church Changes for the Worse

The third reason people leave church is because the church no longer feels like community to them. Perhaps their close friends have left, an important ritual changes, or their season of service has come to an end. Or a change in leadership shakes them up.

One church I served, for instance, saw a mass exodus when a long-time, talented choir director left. Many of the choir members had joined the church because of the choir; making music with this group became their primary expression of faith. The choir served as their small group for both spiritual growth and social connection. When the church brought in a new choir director who was gifted in his own right but didn't do things the way the previous one did, many choir members left.

Some people leave when conflict isn't addressed, reconciliation isn't offered, or forgiveness isn't granted. People also leave when the church doesn't fulfill on its promise to be an inclusive community of love. For instance, some churches are not equipped to effectively integrate and teach children on the autism spectrum.

Other churches send out clues that racism, sexism, or homophobia will or won't be tolerated. Still other churches won't welcome people who don't fit their political, social or theological norms.

Finally, churches change for the worse when mission stops, gossip engulfs the congregation or a breach of trust takes place. If fraud or sexual misconduct occurs, the church will necessarily undergo a difficult period of self-reflection, healing, and change. Many people may leave during the process, unwilling or unable to deal with the shattering aftermath.

Growth of the Spiritual but not Religious Movement

The fourth reason people leave the church is that their beliefs change, or they no longer find answers to their questions there. You could say that the church no longer engages them spiritually. As the Third Great Awakening has been replaced by the Great Decline, religious affiliation has shrunk over the last sixty to seventy years. At the same time, another significant trend has been on the rise: an intense interest in spirituality apart from religion and the growth of the number of people who identify as "spiritual but not religious." When people identify as spiritual but not religious, in essence, they are telling us that they deeply desire to connect with the spiritual aspects of life, but the church isn't providing that vital opportunity. Perhaps the standard worship format of a call to worship, prayer, sermon, pastoral prayer, and offering, and on some Sundays, holy communion or baptism – interspersed with three or four songs – isn't what speaks to them. It's not that the church doesn't talk to and about God; it's that the church doesn't make time for the direct experience of God. For example, have you ever noticed that silent prayer during corporate worship might last only five to ten seconds before the space gets filled with words again? That brief silence in a noisy, crowded week doesn't leave much room to connect with one's own soul or spirit. Or for God to speak to you.

When churches focus on head knowledge to the exclusion of the heart, they run the risk of neglecting spirituality. When expository preaching, debates over *The Book of Discipline*, or protracted conversations about administrative processes get more air time than spending time in God's presence, the church also runs the risk of neglecting spirituality. These risks are real. People are looking for something more substantive and more soulful. In fact, they tell us on the way out the door that they want more spirituality in the church, not less. If the church is not meeting spiritual needs, it needs to evolve.

How Do We Do More with Less?

Churches ask a third persistent question: "How do we do more with less?" This question worried many churches even before the pandemic. In other words, churches already operating from a model of decline were struggling. And the shutdowns simply exacerbated their sense of lack in three areas: togetherness, resources, and the experience necessary to weather dramatic change. While not every congregation has been negatively impacted in all three areas, church leaders share with me that the question of how to do more with less has become urgent in at least one of these areas.

Less Togetherness

Just as we faced the most disorienting set of changes that many of us have ever experienced in a compressed amount of time, we also entered an extended period of imposed isolation. Not being able to assemble in person during the pandemic for worship, Bible study or even coffee put a big dent in our sense of togetherness. It frayed our sense of cohesion precisely when we needed it the most. And the isolation wasn't just from shutdowns. Travel and gathering restrictions left us feeling cut off and alone. Unmoored from our previous rhythms and routines of being with people, we drifted apart. The congregational members we knew and loved to see each week were suddenly absent from our lives.

Dictionary.com defines congregation as "an assembly of persons brought together for common religious worship." Many churchgoers look forward to Sunday worship, knowing they will see friends and family, catch up on the past week, and share the Christian journey through ceremony and ritual; the preached word, song, and prayer; handshakes and hugs; and amens. They know, at least on Sunday mornings, that they are not alone in this world. The natural result, then, of closing church doors is that people lose a feeling of togetherness that, as a congregation, they count on.

As our patterns of congregating and interacting shifted throughout the pandemic, people had to make substantial and intentional efforts to connect with one another, not to mention the efforts each person had to make to adapt to the slew of other changes the pandemic brought. As opportunities to gather in any traditional way diminished and the subsequent sense of connection to each other throughout the shutdowns changed, the ripple effects have been enormous.

The most significant change is that people haven't automatically come back together. Where did everyone go? New schedules and routines, as well as health concerns for themselves and others, have shunted people in new directions – including away from church. With less togetherness and fewer people, including those who died or moved during the pandemic, it's seemed harder to mount mission projects, restart ministries, assemble a choir or launch a children's program.

Even when people are present, there is a lingering sense of absence. If you had been starting from scratch, twenty-five souls in worship might feel like a win. But if you had fifty souls in worship before the shutdowns, twenty-five souls in worship are a whole different story. Missing half your people is a shocking loss. Also, when people worship by way of online technology, even though they're worshiping "with" you, if you can't see them or aren't otherwise aware of the people attending "with" you, you don't benefit from their presence – and they don't benefit from yours. Worshiping at different times compounds the sense of fractured community.

The World of Grief

As of March 2022, six million of our family, friends, and neighbors around the globe have died because of the pandemic, including one million in the United States. This does not include deaths from other causes. At the same time that we've experienced an unprecedented surge in deaths, we've also lost familiar ways of supporting individuals facing death and their grieving family and friends. Early in the pandemic, thousands of people died without visits from loved ones and friends, pastoral calls from their clergy, or familiar rites of passage. Mourners could not say goodbye or mark the passing of loved ones in time-honored ways. Funerals and memorial services, which would typically occur within a week or two, were delayed by a year or more.

Rev. Dr. Imani-Sheila Newsome-Camara explains that in the Black church community, mourners' grief was magnified by the loss of additional cultural touchstones such as the service taking place in their home church with "call and response." Call and response takes place in worship as the speaker or preacher calls out a liberating message, and the congregants respond in the affirmative. "It's just been me at the funeral home with a few congregants. The grief feels so familiar and yet strange because of the displacement from those touchstones." Besides that, church leaders themselves were having their own difficulties. Imani-Sheila admits, "As the clergy person, I was supposed to be the guide, but I was lost too."

When mourners cannot share stories and be comforted by one another, or even have a place to go long afterward, this loss creates a deep sense of dislocation. James Graham described the impact of delaying familiar mourning rituals. "I've realized that when people can't do a burial quickly – whether it's cremation or a corporeal body being put in the ground – there is a real sense of drifting. They don't have any place to go to be anchored to for their grief." When you lose a loved one, grief is hard enough. If you have lost several loved ones, the grief adds up. Grief compounds exponentially when your congregation or community has lost a number of people. Multiple losses without proper mourning created a seemingly never-ending feeling of anguish that people feared would stay with them for years.

Research confirms our need for timely funerals and burials to accept, adjust, and heal from death. For example, a May 2020 study on grief published in

Psychiatry found that "Funeral and burial rituals are important for the effective adjustment of people grieving the loss of a loved one, and mourners who drew comfort from planning and participating in the funeral were shown to achieve better outcomes in later grief." Moving on without appropriate grief rituals – gathering for a service, attending a graveside, or participating in a meal with family and friends – can make a person feel like, without closure, they're leaving their loved one behind without the respect and honor due. Weighed down by unprocessed grief, it's hard to move forward.

Carrying the burden of this kind of loss is not limited to death. Grief comes too when we lose the daily structures that guide our lives, such as a job, a regular schedule, or even the pattern of a daily commute. These structures bring comfort, assuring us that life takes place in worship as the speaker or preacher calls out a liberating message, and the congregants respond in the affirmative. Grief comes too when we lose the daily structures that guide our lives, such as a job, a regular schedule, or even the pattern of a daily commute. These structures bring comfort, assuring us that life can be counted on, pandemic or not. Losing these structures, however, feels like losing control, making grief even more challenging to handle. Whether or not you've lost someone to death during the pandemic, you're among a whole world of people grieving to one degree or another right now.

Fewer Resources

When it comes to doing more with less, the area that sends fear and anxiety through a congregation is having access to fewer resources, ranging from less money to less engagement in mission and ministry to less investment of time and energy.

The fact is that congregations run not only on faith but on finances. When contributions decrease, so does our ability to impact the community for good. Sadly, the question of how we do more with less money isn't new for the church. Churches across the country have been struggling with money issues for many years. Faithful tithers pass away, attendance decreases, and the offering plate takes a hit. The go-to answer usually involves budget cuts, asking members to increase their giving by sharing the church's financial needs, and endless fundraisers. The heartbreaking reality is that without enough money, missions, ministry, and the process of disciple-making gets decreased or eliminated for the sake of payroll, keeping the lights on, and maintaining the building.

Amid financial challenges present before the pandemic, churches never dreamed the day would come when their doors would be closed for more than a week or two. It's one thing to close your doors because of inclement weather; it's a whole new financial challenge to close for one month, two months, six months, or more. Many congregations rely on givers showing up in

REBEKAH SIMON-PETER

person to drop a check in the offering plate. If churches hadn't set up online giving before the pandemic, the opportunity for members to give was likely confusing or missing throughout 2020 and 2021. Even when online giving was set up, churches didn't always know how to encourage people to use it.

Rev. Patrick McPherson, a pastor in Creating a Culture of Renewal® is one among many who can explain why his church had not yet gone fully online with giving: "Our biggest giver is eighty years old. He gives about 20 percent of the church budget. He writes checks, and he's not going to do it." Many faithful members born and raised long before the days of online giving are like this man; I can understand Patrick's reasoning. When the biggest givers aren't willing to give online, leaders are less likely to promote that option. My pastor, Rev. Nancy Boswell, agrees: "Our giving is mostly checks, too. I think that it's the age of our congregation. They either don't trust online giving, or they don't understand how it works." And for this generation, it may also feel like too much of a bother.

If your congregation no longer passes an offering plate, giving might also seem less accessible. For example, in one mid-size congregation, the offering plate that was once passed up and down rows of pews has been replaced by a locked chest with a slit on top that sits on a table near the sanctuary entrance. A PowerPoint slide shown during the offertory announces the three ways a person can give: by placing money in the chest, by giving online through the website, or by setting up an automatic cash withdrawal directly through their bank.

Pioneers (the Silent Generation) and Boomers are the generations most likely to still write checks. For many of them, online giving seems less tangible and less satisfying than placing a check, an envelope, a handful of coins, or a slip of bills into an offering plate. Even for me, church was one of the few places I still wrote a check. I did everything else online, but I didn't want to miss the immediate connection between gratitude and giving that passing the plate engendered. Now I, too, give online.

Thankfully, many Pioneers and Boomers are used to annual pledge drives and give regardless of their weekly attendance. So, while churches need to do more with less money, the situation may not be as bad in the long run as some fear. Most Pioneers and Boomers operate in "subscriber" mode. Just as they pay for the newspaper whether they read every issue or not, they tithe to the church whether they attend each week or not. Their giving comes from a sense of duty, ownership, loyalty to God and the institution, as well as commitment to the community. Younger generations, however, are more likely to give according to the "pay-per-view" mode. They give when they're in church and don't give when they're not. Since the notion of "regular" church attendance has dropped from weekly to monthly or every other month, this too creates a sense of lack.

Although many churches have been collecting less money recently, and although churches cannot function on faith alone, faith has helped people see their way through the pandemic, and faithful creativity will help us see our way into an abundant future beyond lack.

Less Mission Engagement

Collecting less money signals that a church may be less engaged in active mission and ministry, too. The Hartford Institute for Religion Research conducted a broad study on how churches fared during 2021, the second year of the pandemic. In their study of 2,074 churches spanning thirty-eight denominations, a mere 15 percent of regular adult attendees were volunteering in the second year of the pandemic. According to another study by *Faith Communities Today*, that's less than half the number of people who volunteered pre-pandemic. *Faith Communities Today* reported that pre-pandemic, 40 percent of attendees could be counted on to volunteer. Dropping from a 40 to 15 percent volunteer rate is a significant slide.

Unfortunately, while faith-based volunteerism went down, almost one-third of the surveyed churches reported that requests for help – ranging from food to finances and from counseling to spiritual guidance – went up.[8] Why, at a time when need increased so much, did mission engagement decrease? What happened to all the volunteers? The pastors I spoke to explained that when you're used to doing mission by gathering around a potluck or bringing a meal to people on the street, it can be hard to envision new ways of doing outreach and ministry. This dynamic points to an even larger issue: when food, rather than values, dictates how the mission and ministry of the church get accomplished, we're in trouble. "Love thy neighbor as thyself" is easier to say than do, especially when survival is at the forefront of our minds. But what happens when a take-care-of-yourself-first way of being leads to neglecting the community we are called to serve?

Less Time, Energy, and Momentum

From the start of the pandemic, people experienced a shift in priorities. In some cases, this shift created more time and energy, and in other cases, less. Many parents and grandparents enjoyed the extra time with kids and grandkids, yet their lives were unexpectedly disrupted by the expectation to home school while also working from home.

As commitments and schedules radically changed, people simply have not resumed volunteering at pre-pandemic levels with the church. This change means churches with less mission engagement, less time and energy, and less money have one more strike against them: less momentum. If you're not able to build off each other's energy and ideas, you're less likely to create a new vision for the future. When you feel tired or afraid, it's easy to fall into default mode; to go back to what you've known rather than forge a new path. But without a creative, Jesus-like dream, the call to volunteers is just a request to help you regain the past, which, as we've already seen, isn't coming back. It will take all of us to have a Kin(g)dom impact on the community.

Trying to do more with less time, energy, and momentum to engage the life of faith has left many people feeling discouraged and resigned. Especially when churches felt like they were already operating in deficit mode.

Less Experience and Expertise in Adapting to Dramatic Change

Just as major snowstorms and hurricanes test the capacities of communities to respond to dramatic changes in weather, COVID-19 tested the church's capacity to deal with dramatic changes in every aspect of church life. Just about everything that could change during this period of time did. The pandemic required rapid change and an agility not usually demonstrated by the church.

Because churches tend to be oriented toward tradition, the challenge to quickly pivot and adapt to far-reaching change has been especially difficult. The culture of many congregations tends toward stability and harmony. Churches usually prefer to conserve traditions and take their time making changes. Risk-takers are either not attracted to leadership roles in churches that take a measured approach to change, or are not well tolerated. That means that as an institution, we simply have less experience and less expertise adapting quickly to changes as far-reaching and dramatic as a pandemic.

As COVID-19 moved across the world, the church faced questions it couldn't have imagined, such as "How do we do worship if not in our building?" "How do we take up an offering with no one around to give?" "When can we reschedule the potluck for Sunday?" Initial decisions came swiftly. You closed the doors for the sake of the community and moved into the future. The problem was that many churches only fulfilled half the change. While congregations stopped meeting in person, many of them didn't know what to start in its place.

Less Experience with Technology

Since 2007, our lives have been profoundly shaped by technology. That's when the first iPhone hit the market. Even if you didn't own one, this small device made technology an integral part of daily life. It "put the internet in everyone's pocket," boosted platforms like Facebook and Google, and caused chewing gum sales to plummet. Impulse buying at the grocery checkout line dropped as people spent more time on their phones.[9]

With the advent of apps just a year later in 2008, the

smartphone changed how we do almost everything. As big box stores put mom-and-pop shops out of business, so the app store rendered all kinds of separate devices and items unnecessary or obsolete. Do you remember the last time you saw maps for sale at a gas station? Through an app store, you can access everything from maps to a flashlight to the radio on your phone. In addition, today, one phone contains a still camera, a video camera, and photo albums. The smartphone has singlehandedly turned photography from a hobby for the select few to a form of everyday expression. With this same phone, you can bank, shop, and meditate. You can meet with your doctor and supply your own vital signs, including your pulse, heart rate, blood sugar, and calories burned. You can even track your sleep in ways that previously required access to an expensive sleep lab and a night away from home. Using your phone, you can read books, write blogs, and keep up with the news. Most importantly, you can text friends, check your email, and work from practically anywhere in the world. And if you want to, you can make phone calls.

Technology saturates every aspect of our lives. With high-powered computers in our pockets, we no longer dial up to "go online." Instead, we live our lives intricately interconnected to the virtual world. More than 46 percent of those sixty-five and older own a smartphone, while almost 100 percent of eighteen- to twenty-nine-year-olds own a smartphone. The average American, including

Boomers, spends more than five hours every day interacting with their phone, checking it up to sixty-three times every day. Integrating technology into the life of the church is a natural – and necessary – next step.

While many churches went online without any problem during the pandemic, others had a different experience. Perhaps one or two leaders were creatively using online technology to provide worship. While their solutions were much appreciated, these leaders soon experienced burnout as they bravely carried the torch themselves. Surrounded by congregations of people accustomed to taking their time to evaluate and institute change, the question is how does the church as a whole, and with sufficient speed, consistently move forward in the arena of communication and technology?

Sarah Payne reveals, "We still have people in our congregation who don't use email. At the same time, we're trying to reach Gen Z, who use TikTok, Snapchat, and Instagram." These dramatic differences between the way older and younger generations use technology raise this question: How do you do more with less when it comes to technology? The question is especially poignant for older and smaller congregations that don't always have tech-savvy people to incorporate all the gifts technology can bring. Clayton Payne acknowledges, "The digital learning curve is so high that it creates technological apathy among some of our leaders. They're very accustomed to one way of doing ministry, which is not effective right now." The result is that the entire weight of technology may rest on the shoulders of one or two "techies" in the congregation, often the pastor. Other congregations end up having to choose which generations they will serve.

This is a painful inflection point, especially when pastors like Sarah and Clayton know that reaching Gen Z is crucial for the life of the church. The pandemic is this new generation's defining moment; it will forever shape their values, experiences, and sense of the future. "I really have a heart to reach the younger generations," says Sarah. "Even though they continue to separate themselves out from the church, we've got to reach them." That means employing technology in many ways. "But at the same time," notes Sarah, "I still want to express love, care, and concern for those who have faithfully served the church for many, many years." Choosing which generation a church will prioritize feels like a losing proposition all the way around. In this way, technology has, for now, simultaneously become a burden, a barrier, and a blessing.

Medieval Christians Asked the Same Three Questions

Now that we've explored these three persistent questions – When do things go back to normal? How do we get people (back) to church? And, how do we do more with less? – I want you to know that the church has been here before and survived – even thrived. This isn't the first pandemic the church has successfully weathered. In fact, medieval Christians asked the same questions during the time of their era's pandemic – the bubonic plague.

The bubonic plague erupted throughout medieval Europe and lingered for more than three centuries, deeply disrupting all of society, including the church. Based on what I've learned about how the bubonic plague shaped history and how it directly impacted the church, here, in brief, is what I believe would be their answers to these three persistent questions, based on their own experience with the plague.

Q. When do things go back to normal?

A. They don't. Something new had to emerge. For us, that turned out to be the Protestant Reformation.

Q. How do we get people (back) to church?

A. Instead of getting people back to church, we had to go forward, and invite people into something brand new.

Q. How do we do more with less?

A. We tried, but it didn't really work. Trying to fill the gaps left by the plague wasn't very successful. Instead, we had to reorganize the very way we did church.

While there are significant differences between the bubonic plague and the COVID-19 pandemic – not to mention the societies they unfolded in – we share a surprising number of similarities with people of that day.

The good news is that medieval Christians figured it out – just as we will. In the following chapters, I'll show you in greater depth how the plague shaped medieval Christians' answers to these questions and how pandemics, in general, including COVID-19, disrupt life as we know it for good. Most importantly, I'll share what we can learn from the bubonic plague to shape a positive future for the church.

CHAPTER THREE
Pandemics Disrupt for Good

Even as we ask how to get our churches back on their feet and wonder about the best way to move forward, it's important to realize that pandemics disrupt for good. In other words, the disruption is so dramatic that people's ways of living and dying are forever altered. For those of us living through this twenty-first-century pandemic, the days of children sharing toys and school supplies are gone. Gone are the assumptions that all high schoolers will get to play sports, attend dances, go to prom, or learn in a school building. Forget about the notion that everyone will go to work. Work from home, remote learning, and holding meetings online are also not going away. Mask wearing will be more common, as will hand-sanitizing stations. It turns out that coming through a pandemic is chaotic, painful, and messy. It will take a while for the next normal to emerge.

While we wait for this next normal to unfold, it's comforting knowing that good can actually come out of a pandemic. Pandemics disrupt for good by causing surprising progress in medicine, health, economic and social structures, architecture, politics, and religion.

What good has already emerged from the COVID-19 pandemic? Remember when public health officials speculated that there might never be a vaccine? After all, it took nearly 40 years to develop an influenza vaccine and centuries to develop a smallpox vaccine.[10] Yet, within eleven months, scientists from around the globe developed, tested, and brought to market highly effective vaccines. The innovative technology they used was first developed in the 1990s in an ongoing attempt to create an effective way to combat HIV. As this technology was already in use, it cut about four years off the testing and approval process. The genius of female scientists was at the lead.[11] But what was most striking to me was the up-swell of crowd-sourced hope. Symphonies played online, artists offered music and art lessons for free, organizations moved their trainings online. Crowd funding sites raised millions of dollars to support and help hurting people they would never meet. People demonstrated tremendous creativity and generosity. Even as we were stuck at home, telehealth and teletherapy options opened up, so we could attend to each other's well-being. Support for front-line workers grew to include doctors, nurses, restaurant workers, and others who kept society going. Mail-in ballots became commonplace, increasing ease of access to the polls.

The pandemic's disruption – millions of dead, a tenuous hold on daily patterns of life, the suddenness with which our connections were broken, the speed with which they were rejoined online, and the impacts on the church – has me thinking about how to strengthen our connections with one another and with the very spirit of God. In essence, to minimize the long-term effects of these disruptions on our ways of being together, the church must become stronger and more flexible. I have no doubt that communities of faith will last, as they have for millennia, but my question is, *How we can best organize ourselves going forward?* It's time for Christians to get ready for the next normal – and the one after that – by intentionally reimagining the way we do and be church. In fact, we have an extraordinary opportunity before us.

To make the most of this opportunity to grow, strengthen, and expand, Christians can learn a great deal from the bubonic plague that ravaged Europe in the thirteenth to seventeenth centuries, paying close attention to how the church adapted as a result. Studying the plague enables us to anticipate and prepare for the types of changes pandemics can bring, empowering the church to respond quickly, meaningfully, and effectively to the disruptions at hand.

How the Plague Disrupted Europe for Good

The first wave of the bubonic plague lasted from 1347-1351 and wiped out an estimated 25 million people, or 40 to 60 percent of the population of Europe. It arrived in Europe through Sicily in 1347 and moved into mainland Italy, Spain, and France in 1348; it made its way through

Austria, Hungary, Switzerland, and Germany in 1349; then into London, Scotland, and Scandinavia in 1350. The plague wreaked havoc on the entire continent.

Over several centuries, the plague broke out wave upon wave throughout Europe, lasting well into the 1600s.[12] In London alone, it broke out about every ten years over three centuries, killing 20 percent of the population each time.[13] This plague, also known as the "black death," turned whole patches of skin black as it swelled lymph nodes (buboes) in the groin and triggered incessant vomiting, debilitating diarrhea, and piercing headaches. Transmitted by flea bites, the illness was brutal and deadly.

Although written much later, folklorists have connected the nursery rhyme "Ring a Round o' Rosies" to the plague because it describes what happened to those who contracted the highly contagious disease. Remember how it goes? "Ring a round o' rosies / A pocketful of posies / Ashes! Ashes! / We all fall down!"

The "ring a round o' rosies" refers to red rings that first appeared on people's skin, later turning into black boils that led to their so called "black death." People believed the disease was transmitted through terrible smells, so they would hold "a pocketful of [good smelling] posies" to their noses to ward off the plague. "Ashes" refers to dead bodies being burned. The word is sometimes written as "atishoo," mimicking the sound of a sneeze, a symptom common to one variant of the plague. Even today, it's common to bless someone after they sneeze. "We all fall down" refers to the massive number of people who died, and died quickly, sometimes falling to the street dead as they walked.

Even though the phenomenon of pandemics has been around almost as long as farmers have tilled the soil, according to the *Oxford Dictionary,* the term didn't appear in any written records until 1666 when the bubonic plague broke out again in London during one killing summer. The root of the word pandemic traces back to the Greek word pandēmos, meaning "of or belonging to all the people." Unlike an epidemic, which is localized, a pandemic jumps national borders and travels internationally.

In one sense, the pandemic belongs to all of us because we are all impacted by the virus – albeit in a variety of ways. But in another sense, it belongs to us – not as victims of it – but as those who have the power to shape something new from it. For instance, William Shakespeare lived his whole life during outbreaks of the plague when the theater was often closed. Without the rigors of producing and performing, Shakespeare's creativity flourished. Over four years, from 1606 to 1610, London theaters were open just nine months, giving Shakespeare time to write *Macbeth, Antony and Cleopatra, The Winter's Tale,* and *The Tempest.*[14]

Likewise, Sir Isaac Newton, who formulated the

law of gravity, fled to the countryside for a year or two while the plague raged in Cambridge. During this concentrated time away, known as Newton's miracle year, or "annus mirabilis," he made great progress on his lifelong quest to understand "matter, place, time, and motion...the cosmic order, then...light, colors, vision." He lived on his family's childhood farm with apple trees across the way.[15] Watching the apples fall down (rather than up or sideways) from the trees inspired his thinking about gravity and physics, and the plague gave him uninterrupted time to develop more fully his theories of calculus, optics, the laws of motion, and gravity.[16]

"Just as Shakespeare and Newton brought forth new genius from the plague, so people of faith can bring forth new gifts from the pandemic, which I'll discuss at greater length in upcoming chapters.

Stopping the Plague

Although three hundred years is a long time to endure a pandemic, it took that long for medieval society to learn how to contain and then stop the bubonic plague. One of the most effective deterrents was isolating the infected from others so the disease could not spread. When one member of a household contracted the plague, the entire household would then be isolated in their home. Because travelers too carried the plague, ships in harbor came to be isolated for a period of time before people could disembark.[17] Initially, the period of enforced isolation lasted thirty days *(trentino),* but that number expanded to forty days, giving us the word "quarantine" from the Italian *quarantino.* The number forty reflected doctors' evolving understanding of the nature of contagious diseases. For Christians, it also reflected the supposed spiritual nature of the plague. Because people thought the plague was God's will for them, a forty-day quarantine seemed appropriate since Lent, a period of prayer and fasting, was also forty days long.[18]

Over time, people came to understand that the plague spread quickly in crowded settings, including cities. As a result, those who could do so fled to the countryside, practicing an early form of social distancing. While this social distancing kept healthy people safe, it also meant that impacted communities were understaffed. Who would fill civic positions, harvest the fields, give out the sacraments, bury the dead, and keep things going if everyone fled?

Church leaders like 16th century German monk Martin Luther, whose beliefs gave rise to Protestantism, weighed in by encouraging fellow Christians to stay and care for their neighbors, household members, and members of the community, even at great risk to themselves. In 1527 Luther wrote a pamphlet, "Whether One May Flee from a Deadly Plague."[19] Even though Luther thought everything was within God's control (including the plague) and that illness was punishment from God, he also affirmed human responsibility to care for others and condemned those who carelessly infected the people around them.[20]

In addition to quarantining, caring for each other, and fleeing crowded cities for the less crowded countryside, authorities also discovered the value of shutting down large assemblies to slow contagion. Parish records of the Catholic churches were carefully consulted each week to track the death rates. When the weekly death toll rose above thirty souls, authorities forbid mass gatherings – including feasts, archery contests, and the ever-popular theater. On the other hand, churches remained open no matter the rate of death because no one thought they could catch or transmit the plague during the worship of God. Unfortunately, the numbers showed otherwise. "Almost half the diocesan clergy had died during the first plague, and recurring epidemics continued to dwindle the clerical population and prevent it from effectively answering the religious needs of the European Christian population," writes McLaurine H. Zentner in "The Black Death and Its Impact on the Church and Popular Religion."[21]

During the height of the plague in 1349, roughly 45 percent of the priests in ten dioceses throughout England died, with mortality reaching as high as 50 percent in Exeter and Winchester. Priests in the diocese of Barcelona were especially hard hit. Sixty percent of priests there died between 1348 and 1349.

The high rate of death among the clergy and religious workers of the day surprised and terrified people. If the clergy were not immune from this unpredictable wrath of God, who could be? Of course, we know now that their close contact with parishioners made them as susceptible as everyone else to the highly contagious plague. Perhaps even more so, as they heard confessions and administered last rites to the dying. "Priests were faced with the task of stepping into sickrooms, knowing that they faced an unseen enemy that very likely would kill them shortly."[22]

To get a feel for what that must have been like, imagine what would happen to congregations today if a quarter, half, or even more of the clergy, musicians, youth workers, Sunday school leaders, and regional leaders, not to mention the congregants, dropped dead in their duties over the course of a summer, or a year, or two. The life of the church would all but grind to a halt. Church leaders would try to limp along with the people who were left to meet any needs they could but with a greatly reduced presence. At the same time, people's spiritual, emotional, and physical needs would be even greater. In addition to the standard administrative duties in the life of the church, there would be an increased need for pastoral care, guidance, prayer, grief work, funeral services, and a need to calm the immense fears associated with the sudden loss of life and the disintegration of an institution that long connected people with God.

As unimaginable as all this is, that's exactly what happened during the time of the bubonic plague. "The period of The Black Death was a troubling one for members of the religious community, and faith in the Church as an institution was shaken to its core. The public demanded an explanation for the plague all around them, and while there was a sense it might be punishment for sin, there seemed to be no rhyme or reason to it. Confidence in the power of shrines and talismans that had brought comfort for decades was shattered, and fearful priests who shirked their duties were held up as examples of the clergy's failings as a whole. Cloistered communities were the perfect breeding ground for plague, with whole monasteries and abbeys being wiped out. It seemed the Church had no answers, but this did not stop vast amounts of local priests from doing all they could to give their parishioners spiritual solace as they faced their deaths."[22] Not only did the plague itself raise questions about the efficacy of the church, but before the plague even began, church leaders had turned their attention to more secular concerns, such as amassing wealth and cultivating political power. This further weakened their ability to care for the laity once the plague began to spread across Europe.

As you can imagine, the plague had powerful impacts on the way Christians lived out their faith and the way the church sought to organize itself going forward. With such a massive die-off of both clergy and of faith in the institution, the church became unable and untrustworthy to meet the spiritual needs of the people. The lack of a strong, caring, and responsive church led

people to promote their own individualized versions
of faith, which no longer depended on the now absent
church structure. Those who could afford it hired clergy
to conduct private masses and administer the sacraments
in private family chapels. This privatization of spiritual
services was just one workaround. There was also a
rise of lay-led religious orders that bypassed the clergy
altogether. Pilgrimages to holy sites grew in popularity,
as did praying to the saints. These laity-dependent
adaptations were a medieval version of the spiritual but
not religious movement.

Perhaps the most striking lay movement that
arose was the flagellants. These traveling bands of
zealous Christians beat themselves with knotted ropes
to appease what they supposed to be an angry God.
McLaurine H. Zentner writes:

> The European population had never experienced death
> in such numbers, and when they realized that the plague
> spared no one, regardless of their faith or amount of good
> works performed, they grew desperate to find protection
> for their souls.

Even the medical authorities of the time shrugged
their shoulders, offering little hope of relief. They
believed that if the plague was God's will there was
little they could do; Christians realized that neither
the church nor medicine could safeguard them from a
punishing God. Instead, they started to see the flagellant
movement as a solution. Through self-flagellation, these
penitents would intentionally punish themselves before

God could and perhaps thereby invite divine mercy. The flagellants not only practiced self-punishment, but their devastating theology also led to the scapegoating of minorities – whom they also believed were to blame for their difficulties. The flagellants led persecutions and mass killings of Jews, the Roma people, and others.[23]

Meanwhile, the church found its own workarounds for offering encouragement in a terrifying, violent, and hateful time. Not only did popes denounce the flagellant movement and the scapegoating of minorities, the church offered indulgences to people who worried about the state of their soul after they died. These certificates pardoned people for their sins and promised a shorter time in the cleansing suffering of purgatory before entering paradise. In reality, though, the sale of indulgences served as part cottage industry for entrepreneurial clergy whose livelihood was tenuous due to the plague, and only part pastoral care by the church. Either way, Martin Luther argued against indulgences, stating that God granted salvation to all the faithful. In 1517, he wrote his "Disputation on the Power of Indulgences," or The Ninety-Five Theses, against being able to buy or earn forgiveness for sins. Challenges to the Catholic Church like this from Luther, John Calvin, and others led to the Protestant Reformation. The Protestant Reformation allowed Christians to be less dependent on external power structures for their relationship with God, which included being able to directly consult the Bible for spiritual wisdom.[24]

Meanwhile, instead of the traditional religious view that prayer and confession would heal the sin of sickness, doctors and scientists began to sort out the biological sources of disease and offer new ways of healing. Hospitals transformed from places of mere hospitality for the down-and-out to places of physical healing. The power of laughter to heal was also discovered and implemented. Not only did hospitals and the nature of healing evolve, so did the structure of houses. Homes transformed from big, open halls where people and their animals lived together, including uninvited mice and rats, to structures with separate rooms – an early form of architectural social distancing.

The sheer number of people killed by the plague broke apart the structure of feudal society, which consisted of clergy as mediators of divine order, paralleled by a monarch whose nobles were the landowners. Next in the power structure came knights, who were considered mighty warriors. Next came the commoners. This free class included farmers, merchants, tradesmen, and craftsmen. At the very bottom of the structures of power were serfs, peasants, and slaves. These laborers were generally bound to the land of their owners or overlords, paid taxes and tithes, and had little to no freedom to direct their own lives and futures.

But as the plague rolled across Europe and the death toll of serfs, peasants, and slaves rose, reliable sources of labor disappear, changing the dynamics of power outside the church. For the first time, serfs could bargain and demand better treatment, including payment for their labor. This unexpected shift led to the rise of Western individualism, and ultimately, to the middle class. At the same time, surviving clergy, who had always been woefully underpaid, also gained new bargaining power.

Parallels between the Bubonic Plague and COVID-19

Stretching over three centuries, the bubonic plague forever changed medieval society in Europe. In the midst of it, very few people if any, could have predicted the substantial shifts in economic and social structures that would lead to new freedom and power for various classes of people. Even today, we're benefiting from the remarkable innovations in science, economics, medicine, and theology that the bubonic plague brought about.

Although the bubonic plague erupted over the course of three centuries and COVID-19 will likely last no more than three years, both pandemics share three striking parallels from which we can learn. First, the medieval church was weakened by a quest for wealth, power, influence, and an alliance with politics long before the plague impacted it. This pre-existing condition revealed the need for greater spirituality in the church and gave rise to a medieval version of the spiritual but not religious movement. The church today has a similar pre-existing condition and a contemporary version of the spiritual but not religious movement.

Second, the changing world of work brought on by the plague in medieval days is similar to the changes we are experiencing now. These changes can teach the church about the need to build spiritual community. At the same time, the Platinum Rule, a twist on the Golden Rule, can heal polarization. I'll discuss this more later.

Third, plague-era technologies greatly expanded access to knowledge and introduced a new way to connect with others and to share ideas with greater velocity. Similarly, pandemic-era technologies today expand communication and increase our connections in surprising ways.

Rev. Ben David Hensley, a participant in Creating a Culture of Renewal®, frames it this way:

> The "church" is being forced to confront its mortality in light of what all of us are becoming aware of during this pandemic – namely that we are hungry for real community, real spiritual connection with the divine, and real meaningful work in our communities. We just aren't getting that, generally, from the "church." Why is our bar so low?

I agree with Ben's take on our current situation. In the church, we've resigned ourselves to the culture of decline and believe that there's not much we can do to change societal forces that impact the church. COVID-19 added to our resignation. But protecting ourselves by setting low expectations doesn't represent what Jesus called us to do as his followers or his ambassadors.

In fact, I believe this is our moment. Jeremy Gutsche notes that after the chaos of every pandemic comes an unprecedented era of creativity and innovation. The Renaissance came after the bubonic plague. The Roaring 20's came after the flu pandemic of 1918. The next era of innovation, which Jeremy Gutsche calls the Roaring 2020's, is unfolding before us even now. Now is the time for the church to take advantage of the momentum the pandemic has brought by incorporating three key culture shifts into its way of being.

These culture shifts also speak to the three persistent questions we addressed earlier – questions raised by medieval Christians, as well as Christians today.

Q: When do things go back to normal?

A: Embrace spirituality and the next normal

Q: How do we get people (back) to church?

A: Invite people (back) to church as community

Q: How do we do more with less?

A: Adopt the culture of technology to do more with less

CHAPTER FOUR

Embrace Spirituality and the Next Normal

The Spiritual but Not Religious

In the quest to return to normal many church leaders and members are operating from the assumption that the church as-is can grow past the impacts of the pandemic. These churches believe once the pandemic is over, we'll go back to something recognizable. They believe, in the meantime, we need to get our programs back up and running, offer a full calendar, and go invite people! Canvas the neighborhood, knock on doors, leave flyers, send out invitations, and then wait for people to show up.

While there is some validity to this approach, it misses the innovative opportunities before us. This is the perfect time to learn from medieval Christians and pandemics past to align ourselves with God's unfolding future. It's time to envision a new path forward beyond putting the coffee pot back on for the fellowship hour, and passing the offering plate.

As I've said, before waves of the bubonic plague rolled across Europe, the church had already shifted some of its focus from the care of souls to gaining political power and amassing wealth. Religious and political leaders formed alliances similar to marriages of convenience to achieve their individual goals. This focus on political power weakened the spiritual power of the church by diverting its attention from the care of bodies and souls to worldly matters.

As the plague decimated the ranks of the clergy, the church trained new priests, but many of them were young, poorly educated, and ill-equipped to serve people well. People were left to find their own way to safeguard their souls from the plague they believed was a sign of the wrath of God.

While still identifying as Catholic, because no other form of Western European Christian faith expression existed until the Protestant Reformation of 1517, people went around the church authorities and structures to create new ways of connecting to God. The development of the Reformation itself was an example of this yearning for more direct spiritual connection.

I used to think that the rise of the spiritual but not religious movement – people who were once associated with the church but left to pursue their relationship with God on their own terms – was a twentieth- and twenty-first-century phenomenon. But it's clear to me now, looking back at how people responded to the plague, that this movement began much earlier than I ever suspected.

The medieval church was not the only iteration of

church that was weakened by aligning itself with politics. The American church of today is in a similar position. It was also already weakened by partisan politics before the pandemic came. U.S. churches have aligned themselves at various points across the political spectrum. Churches with more conservative theologies tend to align with the Republican Party, while churches with more liberal theologies tend to align with the Democratic Party. As political parties have grown farther apart, so have church members and denominations. This polarization has made it hard for Christians to agree on a shared meaning of the Gospel since they're now inclined to interpret the Bible through the lens of their political party's platform. Political leaders of different parties used to work together despite their differences. But this kind of bipartisanship has been increasingly replaced by win/lose politics. This same uncompromising attitude has made its way into churches as well, making it hard for the church body to act in a united way. While Jesus himself, not to mention Martin Luther and John Wesley, challenged the reigning politics of the day, churches today seem rather to be manipulated by politics. Disenchanted with the church's alignment with a politics of division rather than an ethics of love, many people had left the chruch even before the pandemic hit.

As I noted before, even as religious affiliation has dropped over the years, spiritual affiliation has dramatically increased. This phenomenon has been

connected to the growth of twelve-step groups such as
Alcoholics Anonymous, that bill themselves as spiritual
but not religious. The de-emphasis on religion has
allowed people of many religious backgrounds, or none
at all, to come together for a common purpose, to recover
from alcoholism. Yet, in Alcoholics Anonymous, there is
a deep reliance on God. Alcoholics learn that in order to
recover from alcoholism, they must develop a profound
connection with a Power greater than themselves; this
connection must go deeper even than what is typically
found in church. While traditional church worship and
Bible study points to the Spirit, it doesn't ask much of
the worshiper. Yet, working the twelve steps requires
emotional and spiritual rigor, transparency, and
authenticity, which leads to miraculous growth and a
willingness to serve.

Alignment with politics isn't the only reason people
leave organized religion. Another common reason given
is that churches are seen as judging the world rather than
offering the love of God. Rather than feeling closer to God
by coming to church, people have felt more disconnected.
Given that the Bible itself is chock full of examples of
spiritual experiences, this sense of distance is tragic.

Spirituality in the Bible

If you open up a Bible, you'll see a plethora of ways
that God has symbolically and historically interacted
with humanity. Consider the well-known biblical figures

and their stories found throughout the Bible. Each of these stories tells of an encounter with God.

In Genesis, Adam and Eve speak with God in the garden, Abraham and Sarah entertain angels, Jacob wrestles with an angel, and Joseph experiences divinely inspired dreams.

In Exodus, Moses sees a supernatural sight when he spots a bush that burns but is not consumed, he hears the voice of God and has many interactions with God on Mt. Sinai, and Israel has miraculous experiences in the desert.

In the books of the prophets, Hannah's prayers are answered in a miraculous way; her son, Samuel, hears the call of God; Elijah becomes aware of the still small voice of God; the prophet Elisha causes miraculous provision for the widow; Ezekiel sees a vision of dry bones rise up and become whole again.

In the Gospels, Zechariah, Mary, and Joseph each have encounters with messengers of God; Mary has a sacred and unexpected encounter with the Spirit upon Jesus' conception; Joseph receives divine guidance through his dreams; Jesus is ablaze with light on the Mount of Transfiguration; people experience a wide range of miraculous healings in Jesus' presence; Peter walks on water.

In the book of Acts, the apostles experience a sudden outpouring of the Spirit at Pentecost, Jews from every nation miraculously understand a common language,

Peter is sprung from jail through the power of prayer, and Paul has life-altering experiences on the road to Damascus.

This list is far from definitive or comprehensive, but you get the idea. The God of the Bible is a God of direct encounters. But, over the centuries, people of faith have taken this record of spiritual experiences and mined them for morals, lessons, and do's and dont's. We have recast these spiritual experiences as religious experiences by focusing on the beliefs and behaviors derived from them rather than the transcendent states being described in them. As a result, sometimes even church people think that a direct experience of God is out of reach.

But as Sharon Janis writes in *Spirituality for Dummies:*

> *One of the great gifts of spiritual knowledge is that it realigns your sense of self to something you may not have even ever imagined was within you. Spirituality says that even if you think you're limited and small, it simply isn't so. You're greater and more powerful than you have ever imagined. A great and divine light exists inside of you. This same light is also in everyone you know and in everyone you will ever know in the future. You may think you're limited to just your physical body and state of affairs – including your gender, race, family, job, and status in life – but spirituality comes in and says, "there is more than this."* [25]

Rather than fearing or dismissing the message that the spiritual but not religious communicate by leaving the church, let's learn from them instead.

They're signaling the need for a shift in church culture we can all benefit from. As we pay attention, I think we'll find that the news is generally hopeful. People want to experience God. They want to experience the transcendent. People want more of church, not less.

As you move the church forward in this post-pandemic world, this is the perfect time to lead people to refocus on the spiritual aspects of the Bible, and to encourage divine encounters in their life. Not just to learn about Jesus but be in the presence of Jesus. Not just to hear stories in sermons about transcendent experiences but to experience their own.

A recent graph in Christian Century magazine showed that when it comes to the spiritual but not religious category, about an equal number of people moved into that category as moved out of it. In other words, some people opted to be spiritual *and* religious. They found what they were looking for in organized religion, in church. At the same time, others did not. They declared themselves done with church.

This shift in religious practice is not isolated. In fact, it fits well with two larger cultural trends. In the first cultural trend, people with some discretionary spending now value experience over material goods. They would rather spend money going to a NASCAR race, a sister's trip, or a destination wedding than buy a larger house or a more luxurious car. Jeremy Gutsche, who discerns future trends, underscores the trend: "In a world abundant with stuff, experience becomes a more important currency and life priority." In the second cultural trend, people value the quality of genuineness in communication over slick messaging. Gutsche notes, "Social media and a resistance to traditional advertising have created a desire for authenticity and reality."[26]

When you put these two trends together, experience and genuineness, you get good news for the post-pandemic church. People want to experience themselves as spiritual beings, and they want to have a direct and personal connection with the divine. What an opening for the church! This trend calls to mind the origins of the church itself. When people met Jesus, they felt a connection to God. They not only witnessed miracles in his presence, the disciples were even trained in co-creating miracles. People are still hungry for this kind of experience. Our biology contains the proof.

People are Built for Relationship with God

Even as in-person worship was deemed nonessential during the height of the pandemic, it turns out that prayer was absolutely essential. A scientific study of Google searches during the first three months of the pandemic for the ninety-five most religious countries of the world, encompassing 68 percent of the global population, showed the highest spike ever in searches for prayer. A Pew

Research Center survey demonstrates that 55 percent of the U.S. population prayed for an end to the coronavirus, while a survey conducted by the University of Denmark[27] demonstrates that 55 percent of the global population also prayed for an end to the coronavirus.

Faith-based community flourished online as well. When we realized we couldn't be together in person during the pandemic, people were willing to do whatever it took to create forms of online togetherness. Worship, Bible study, prayer groups, meditation groups, twelve-step groups, and other forms of religious and spiritual community popped up all over the internet.

This makes sense. As the historical record shows, people have participated in religious and spiritual communities for millennia. No matter how advanced or scientifically oriented we become, spirituality and religious community still matter.

In recent years, scientific studies have undertaken the quest to discover why this is. Is the bent toward spirituality or religiosity simply cultural? Is it biological? In other words, is this a matter of nature or nurture?

It turns out that an increasing number of studies demonstrate that a yearning for the transcendent is basic to our biological makeup. It is hardwired into our very being. Consider the following three studies.

In 2018, neurobiological studies conducted at both Yale and Columbia universities demonstrated that our brains are wired to transmit both logical and rational data as well as spiritual and transcendent processes. Interestingly, these transmissions travel along different neural pathways and occupy distinct parts of the brain. In other words, we are not built for one or the other. Instead, our brains have dual capacities. In fact, both the logical and the spiritual are needed for our full functioning. These results proved true for subjects whether they considered themselves spiritual or religious or not.[28]

The Yale and Columbia studies built upon an earlier study that confirmed that no one single area of the brain can be identified as a "God spot." Rather, responses to religious or spiritual phenomena are distributed throughout the brain. "We have found a neuropsychological basis for spirituality, but it's not isolated to one specific area of the brain," confirmed Brick Johnstone, professor of health psychology at the University of Missouri School of Health Professions. "Spirituality is a dynamic concept that uses many parts of the brain. Certain parts of the brain play more predominant roles, but they all work together to facilitate individuals' spiritual experiences."[29]

Studies on the brain's role in spirituality have largely used functional MRI scans – showing that certain brain areas "light up" when people envision a previous spiritual experience. But, a third study sought to clarify the nature of these neural pathways. In other words, were the neural pathways that lit up when spiritual experiences were being remembered simply correlated with these experiences or were they actually the source of them? The study, conducted at the Center for Brain Circuit Therapeutics at Brigham and Women's Hospital in Boston, suggests that anyone can have these kinds of experiences, regardless of religiosity or religious affiliation.[30]

These three studies point to the essential nature of spirituality within humans. Maybe this is why people who no longer relate to church or weren't raised in church still insist on being spiritual even if they are no longer religious.

Not only are we humans built for a relationship with God, but it's natural for us to grow and evolve in our understanding of and relationship with God. In fact, formal studies of faith development show that the movement from identifying as religious to identifying as spiritual can be a natural part of the progression of faith development. Much like human physical development has been shown to follow a predictable process, the same is true with faith development, regardless of the content or the context of the faith. Also, as with physical development, a person does not necessarily progress through all the stages of faith.

Stages of Faith Development

James Fowler was a Professor of Theology and Human Development at Emory University who created a six-part model of the stages in a person's faith journey.[31] This model, based on hundreds of life stories, can help us make sense of the spiritual but not religious movement in a way that inspires hope, rather than discouragement. Let's take a closer look.

Fowler's first stage (intuitive-projective) is one in which fantasy and reality mix. Preschoolers pick up ideas about God from parents and society at large. In the second stage (mythic-literal) school-age children begin to understand logic. But they still accept stories told in literal ways.

Fowler's third stage (synthetic-conventional) begins in the teenage years. Here, young people develop an all-encompassing belief system that synthesizes what they know about the world from school, friends, family, church, after school groups, and/or work. Even as they unconsciously form their belief system, they are unaware that they have a system or that different systems exist, shaped by the life experiences of others. This belief system provides a sense of stability, identity, and belonging. Trust is placed in individuals or groups that best represent their belief system. Fowler notes that many people remain in this stage throughout their lives.

Fowler's fourth stage (individuative-reflective) can begin to unfold as early as young adulthood. Here, awareness expands and the realization dawns that their belief system is but one of many. As the person engages critical exploration of their own system of thinking, disillusionment with their beliefs may begin. In this case, the person may become disenchanted with their community or religion and swing to the opposite extreme to identify as nonreligious. "Ironically the stage three people usually think that stage four people have become 'backsliders' when in reality they have actually moved forward."[30]

In Fowler's fifth stage (conjunctive faith), rarely begun before mid-life, the limits of logic are acknowledged as the paradoxes of life are accepted and integrated. At this time, a person may return to the stories of faith but in a symbolic, more universal way. Fowler notes that both logic and faith can come together in this stage without compromising either one. At this stage of faith, a person's understanding of truth expands to encompass both belief and disbelief, paradox and mystery. At this stage, people no longer see faith as a set of black-and-white propositions or a set of either/or dynamics. Instead, they are able to embrace the complexities of life.

Although rarely reached, Fowler's stage six (universalizing faith) takes place when people live their lives in service to others with a faith that transcends religious categorizations. This person operates at the level of universal and unconditional love as their focus shifts from individual concerns to the community's needs at large. Jesus, Bishop Desmond Tutu, Tich Nat Hahn,

the Dalai Lama, Mother Theresa, and Rabbi Zalman
Schacter-Shalomi are examples of this kind of faith.

According to Fowler's model of faith development,
spiritual but not religious folks likely fit into the fourth
stage of faith development because "those who break
out of the previous stage [stage three] usually do so
when they start seriously questioning things on their
own." I often hear people say, "I don't know what people
who don't have a church home do." Yet, the spiritual
but not religious feel free to explore and create new
community, released from the constraints of religious
answers that no longer make sense to them. Just like
the previous stages, people in stage four may stay in
this non-religious mode permanently.

But what if people didn't have to leave the church
in order to grow spiritually? What if churches
intentionally provided an environment for people
to advance in their faith from stage three to four to
five, while remaining in the same congregation? The
spiritually inclined could grow in place at church as
congregations embrace the spiritual journey as the next
normal. I believe churches can incorporate spiritual
formation into worship, Bible study, and mission for
people to explore and express their own relationship
with God more fully.

How do we design our churches for people to
participate in their own spiritual growth? In the next

section, we'll look at four models of spiritual formation and faith development that point the way. Read on to learn how churches can incorporate the spiritual journey into their corporate lives.

Four Models of Spiritual Formation

Let's explore four different models of spiritual formation that congregations can adapt and adopt into their particular community. These include the small group model, the twelve-step model, the group spiritual direction model, and the covenant group model.

Small Group Model

The first model of spiritual formation is the small group model. This model is especially helpful if you already have Bible study or growth groups, and they are open to shifting how they interact. To deepen a focus on spiritual formation, start by developing shared expectations that open up into the spiritual realm. These expectations might include the following: God is ready, willing, and able to speak to each person in new and unique ways; each person can experience the presence of God; and spiritual encounters are not limited to biblical times. In addition, it will be important to let go of pre-defined ways that God might appear or impact a person, or what their response to God should be. In the Bible, God's appearances were surprising, unprecedented, and deeply personal. Assume that God is still free to act in new and unique ways.

Be sure to emphasize the importance of confidentiality so people can self-reveal without fear. Put practices in place to ensure the group remains gossip-free and judgment-free. Within these expectations and values, group members will likely be less guarded and more open to the movement of the Spirit, the active companionship of Christ, and the presence of God.

Use any of a number of small group guides for spiritual formation. Then, train small group leaders to live into the group's new expectations themselves. Building a group culture that embraces the spiritual journey requires intentionality, sensitivity, and care. It also requires accountability. For spirituality as the next normal to permeate the congregation, a church could invite and expect all members to participate in small groups like this.

Twelve-Step Model

Alcoholics Anonymous came out of the Oxford Groups founded in 1921 by Lutheran minister Frank Buchanan. Over the last century, the twelve-step model has blossomed into hundreds of different applications dealing with every addiction and hang-up possible. Alcoholics Anonymous is a non-expert model of mentoring or discipleship, where one person (a sponsor) walks another through the twelve steps as they discover the need to be honest about one's life and limitations (step one) all the way to a spiritual awakening that results in a life of service to others (step twelve). Twelve spiritual principles are woven into the twelve steps, including honesty, hope, faith, courage, integrity, willingness, humility, love, discipline, patience/ perseverance, awareness, and service.[27]

The purpose of the twelve steps is to develop a growing dependence on a Higher Power, a power greater than oneself. This power is not defined doctrinally. Rather, it is "God as you understand Him [sic]." This open-ended approach eliminates fights over doctrine and who is right or wrong. As each person will have different experiences of spiritual growth, variety is both welcomed and accepted in the group setting. Conformity is not required. In this process, humility is deeply valued and reflected through humor and honesty, owning one's mistakes, and growing in an understanding of God's will.

A number of good books help translate this model for use in churches. Additionally, recovery-based churches have formed that incorporate elements of anonymous recovery programs with a Christian-based worshiping community. The rigorous nature of the twelve steps is often compared to the Daily Examen of Ignatian spirituality. Celebrate Recovery is a popular Christ-centered adaptation of the twelve-step model.

Group Spiritual Direction Model

"When did the sermon become a transmission of information rather than an opportunity for spiritual transformation?" That's the question Rev. Tadd Kruithoff of Missouri wrestled with. "I realized that the worship of God is good," he told me, "but a personal experience of God's presence in worship is even better." Tadd wanted everyone to have that experience. But how? He turned to the tradition of spiritual direction for help. This tradition has a long history within the church, but Tadd noted that it's often seen as a side gig rather than the main gig. For instance, if a person wants to learn more about what God is saying to them, they would meet with a trained spiritual director in a series of one-on-one, private sessions.

Tadd decided to try something different. He introduced the model of group spiritual direction into the heart of the worship experience. Each week he intentionally invites the church to listen for what God is saying to them throughout the liturgy, hymns, and sermon, and then to choose their own response. "God is always inviting us," he tells them. "How would we respond if we recognized the invitation?"

When it comes time for worshipers to respond to God's invitation, Tadd doesn't set out a menu of choices. Instead, he trusts the process to unfold organically between each person and God. He found that people step into things much more easily this way than if the church were to develop a list of set programs.

The model of group spiritual direction approach has revitalized worship. "I can't wait to hear what the Spirit has to say to me today," has become a common refrain. This model has also revitalized the church as a whole. When they began this process just nine months ago, the average age of the congregation, which was founded in the 1800s, was 56 years old; they were in the hole financially; the congregation was split on important issues; and they were on the verge of giving up. Since beginning the group spiritual direction model of worship, people began inviting friends to church again, the average age of the congregation has dropped to 40 years old, their money issues have straightened out, and people are finding what they are looking for: a deep connection to God. People say things like, "I think we're going to make it! God is here; God cares about us; God is actually doing something."

The best part of the group spiritual direction model is that it's a pressure-free, guilt-free approach for the church as a whole – both the pastor and the people. God is present, God is active, God is in charge. An added benefit is that process works well in both hybrid and in-person worship settings.

Once you integrate the group spiritual direction model into the life of your church, it can naturally spread out beyond the worship service. Since God is always inviting us, and we are always welcomed to respond, this process can work in administrative settings, Bible studies, and mission events.

Covenant Group Model

The last model for spiritual growth is the covenant group model. This model shares several qualities with the small group model, such as a desire to experience the presence of God and a willingness to be authentically transparent. The covenant group model, however, is structured according to four questions. These queries provide the space to dive beyond one's everyday life into the realm of the soul.

1. **How is it with your soul?** The starting place of the journey is honesty. Check in with your inner being, the wellspring from which life flows that provides a direct connection with God. When all of the world's demands and distractions are moved aside, what is left? Your answer may vary from week to week, from overflowing with grace and gratitude to empty and dry. Each time the group meets, you again start with this question: How is it with your soul? Over time, you will notice that the state of your soul may not coincide with your everyday life. You could be on top of the mountain and feel your soul weary, or be down in the valley with a soul that is overflowing with joy.

2. **Where have the challenges been?** As you move to the second question, vulnerability joins honesty in the conversation. In the days of John Wesley, this question was the time for covenant group members to share where they were struggling. Your struggles might be continued challenges with a relationship or a new temptation that has arisen since the group last met. Sharing your challenge is the first step to loosening its grip on your life. Confidentiality is a must.

3. **Where have the joys been?** After honesty and vulnerability comes celebration. Share where God is at work in your life. There is no limit to where God's presence can be found. It may be a simple smile at the right time or a life-changing and unexpected shift to a better life. To see the Kin(g)dom of God around and within you, simply stop and notice. Give thanks for God's never-ending presence.

4. **What would you like to be held accountable for?** The covenant group process begins with honesty, deepens to vulnerability, rises to celebration, and finally ends with accountability. Accountability is a way of affirming, "Please hold me to my commitment. Ask me the hard questions when I fail to follow through, and rejoice with me when I succeed."

Participating in a covenant group is a powerful choice to put oneself in the space of discovery, the experience of spiritual connection, and the flow of God's unconditional love.

Tips for Embracing Spirituality

As you incorporate the spiritual journey into the life of the church, be encouraged. There is no wrong way to deepen one's spirituality. Begin the journey of gaining buy-in for the process by reading this chapter of the book with other members of the church. Listen for how God speaks to you as you read and discuss with others. Let the Spirit guide you in selecting one of the four models of spiritual formation. Don't be in a rush to choose, as God may prompt each of you in different ways. As you embrace spirituality as the next normal, you will grow in your own relationship with God. Whichever of the four models of spiritual growth you choose, you will be invited to an important place, the core of who you are. May this be a joyous journey of discovery.

Our Identity in Christ

At its very best, the Christian religion reminds us of our identity in Christ, a truth spoken often in the letters of the New Testament. Paul and the other writers reminded their listeners that, through their baptism and belief, they were now children of God. The spiritual journey, which we see can unfold within a religious community, will move beyond head knowledge of your identity as a child of God into heart and soul knowledge of that identity. Cultivating your spirituality opens you to a direct encounter with God. Spirituality is learning and experiencing how important you are to God, how you are made in God's image, and how God created you for community with God and with others. Therefore, I offer that the purpose of the four models of spiritual growth (small group model, twelve-step model, group spiritual direction model, and the covenant group model) is for you to return to your true identity as child of God.

At first, you may see and experience a new connection with God as you participate in one or more of these models of spiritual growth. Wonderful! Live in that moment and celebrate every experience as it comes. On the other hand, you may struggle to hear God's voice and feel God's presence. Don't give up! Know that you are on a journey with God. Each experience, whether you are on cloud nine with God or wondering if God is present, is on the path to a deeper relationship with God.

As your journey continues, you will begin to see that being in the presence of God is not limited to certain times or events. You will come to know that, like Jesus, you are always in the presence of God. Your awareness of your connection with the Divine will become increasingly consistent and, ultimately, second nature. As your church forges a new path and moves forward into the post-pandemic world, let your deepened spirituality shape the path ahead and draw you into new community.

CHAPTER FIVE

Invite People Back to Church as Community

The Changing World of Work

People are hungry for community. We see this in the changing world of work. In fact, the changes to the world of work brought on by the bubonic plague in medieval days are similar to the changes we're now experiencing as a result of COVID-19. As painful as they are, these changes can teach the church about the need to build spiritual community. To answer the question of how to get people back to church, let's take a closer look at the shifts that happened in the workplace then and now.

The bubonic plague deeply impacted the medieval economy. With an estimated one-third of Europe killed by successive waves of the deadly illness, the structure of the feudal system was significantly undermined. Power shifted from local feudal lords, who controlled the destinies and quality of life of all on their manor, to the commoners. These structural and economic shifts gave rise to the first stirrings of a middle class. Rather than being nameless worker bees on a medieval manor who were beholden to the local lord, serfs gained a new sense of choice and enjoyed new freedom. Even underpaid clergy benefited from these shifts as they gained new bargaining power.

The aftermath of the plague gave both serfs and clergy an opportunity to shape their lives and working conditions in a way that had never been possible before. Those who previously had little self-determination could now use their voices – and feet – to improve their lives. As a result, working conditions changed, pay went up, and the dignity and rights of the individual came into view. Out of the chaos of the bubonic plague came the reordering of society and the rough beginnings of capitalism.

During the COVID-19 pandemic, with one million dead in the U.S. alone, we too are experiencing the reordering of our economy and the way we work. When communities shut down to slow the spread of COVID-19, nonessential workers were put on hold. As large numbers of people stayed home from work – because of the comprehensive restrictions that gripped the country for the better part of a year – people began to wonder if they wanted or could afford to work. Those with small children at home weighed the cost of childcare against the potential income from work, determining whether they could afford to both work and pay for childcare. At the same time, those who collected unemployment and stimulus checks gained some unexpected income. Some paid off debts. Others reassessed their lives. Some relaxed for the first time in a long time. Individuals got to consider where, when, and how they wanted to work.

In the early days of the shutdowns, my friend Lyna, a realtor in Denver, could not show houses for four months. During that long, slow stretch of time, she cooked dinner for her mom and sisters each night and got to know her family all over again. "I might have the post-shutdown blues," she confided as the four months came to an end. "I don't want to go back to my crazy schedule of always working; I never saw my family."

Those who worked from home found they could be as productive as they were at the office while being a lot more relaxed. Commuting from the bedroom to the kitchen table gave them extra time to manage the well-being of kids, pets, and parents. It gave them a sense of being present to their whole lives all at once. While boundaries were tough to maintain, the stronger family connections were worth it. When the economy opened back up and it was time to go back to work, a surprising shift had taken place. Many people found they didn't want to spend as much time away from their families or homes in exchange for low wages, unsafe working conditions, or no benefits. They didn't want to give away all their time for work. They wanted a more integrated life with more passion and more downtime.

Holly, who works for a healthcare recruiting firm, was squeezing a few hours of work into her vacation when I met her on Focusmate, a co-working app (another sign of the changing nature of work). She follows up on resumes to see if the people who submitted them actually want to work. "We have had our best year ever because employers are paying us to find people. The question is: will we find them? In the field of healthcare, we need people to go to work to touch others. But mostly people want to work from home."[32] Or, in Holly's case, from the beach.

While some people opt to work from home, others are opting out of work altogether. When employers began hiring again, imagine their surprise when people didn't flock back to work. People in every field were more intentional about how and where they spent their time, especially for their jobs. Once they evaluated their work environment, pay, and expectations, many were ready for something better. This trend became known as the Great Resignation.[33] With three million more jobs than people to fill them, employees had leverage not seen in forty years.[34] "There's now a greater ability for people to fit work into their lives, instead of having lives that squeeze into their work," said Anthony Klotz, associate professor of management at Texas A&M University who coined the term the Great Resignation.[35]

Even pastors are joining the Great Resignation. Melissa Florer-Bixler writes:

> For decades, church people assumed their pastors' commitment to the church would supersede any bruising

and bullying those congregants doled out. I am grateful for my colleagues who are putting this myth to rest by resigning from churches that refuse to provide them the support and care they need to thrive in ministry[36].

The pandemic has given workers the opportunity to step out of a "put up with anything for a paycheck" box and, instead, use their agency to determine and choose the trajectory of their lives.

Work from Home and The Great Resignation Impact the Church

The pandemic-inspired changes in the world of work have now impacted the world of worship. As people reassess their work commitments, they are also reassessing their church commitments. Worship attendance, already in decline before the pandemic, continues to fall. It's like the work-from-home movement and the Great Resignation have now gone to church. Some people are choosing to worship from home while others have resigned from church altogether.

Just as people are rejoining the world of work on their terms – finding jobs with better pay, better benefits, and more fulfilling work – the opportunity is there for people to also realign with church. But first, churches are discovering that they need to be as responsive to these pandemic-era changes as businesses. Just as the workplace has had to pivot to provide the kind of positive work environment, compensation, and benefits that entice people to work, so the experience of worship, fellowship, and Bible study must be worth it for people to invest their time, talents, and treasure. Think about it. If people quit jobs because they don't feel fulfilled, they can just as easily quit church if they don't feel spiritually fulfilled there. In fact, as we have seen, leaving churches that don't address the need to grow spiritually may be an important stage in healthy faith development.

But just as churches can adapt and provide the right environment for people to advance from one stage of faith development to the next, so churches can expand into spiritual communities that meet more needs for more people.

Remember that people are built for relationship with God at a cellular level; we are hardwired for spirituality. People will absolutely participate in church if the experience speaks to them. But if the experience of church feels rote, uninspired, or disconnected from either real life, or the life of the Spirit, then people will be less likely to return.

Just as work environments now have to address themselves to the whole person, churches do too. As I've said before, people want more from church – more vision, more love, more miracles, and more connectedness – not less. They want church to feel more like true community, a place that is sensitive to and inclusive of the whole person, their families, and the complexities of life. Thanks to the pandemic, it's a beautiful time to forge a new path forward, moving from simply being a group of worshipers to being a group of worshipers who live in authentic community.

The Creating a Culture of Renewal® faculty body is practicing the art of creating true spiritual community. Before the pandemic, half a dozen of us crisscrossed the country several times a year to lead cohorts in three-day retreats for leadership development and spiritual formation. With the pandemic, we have moved all our retreats online. At the same time, the faculty body has almost doubled. While church people may fear that the online environment does not promote genuine relationships, we have shown that real relationship and community are not only possible, they are happening. How? We are intentionally guided by our shared commitment to live by and into our faculty covenant: "We covenant to proactively communicate with honesty and vulnerability, rise to 100 percent integrity, cultivate our well-being through accountability and action, and break new ground." These four short phrases guide our work together and lead us into deep self-reflection and soul-care. Out of that we experience deep spiritual community with one another.

Every time we gather online as faculty, we reflect on our covenant. We have found that it impacts us not only as leaders in Creating a Culture of Renewal® but it shapes our personal lives. At least once a year, we gather for a week or more of spiritual formation, leadership

development, and fun. We worship together, study
Jesus' apostolic model, and stretch each other. What has
transformed us from simply being a group of leaders with
a common goal into a true spiritual community? Our
shared commitment to spiritual growth, through honesty,
vulnerability, celebration, and accountability – all given
and received in unconditional love. Like the small group
model, we model what we expect from others. Like the
twelve-step model, we freely share our experience,
strength, hope with each other. Like the group spiritual
direction model, we trust that God is speaking to us. Like
the covenant group model, we relish questions.

Building Spiritual Community

What does spiritual community look like for your
church? And how is it different from what we think of
as church today? A peek into the community that Jesus
formed with his circle of closest friends, known as The
Twelve, can give us a good idea. Jesus and the twelve
disciples spent three intense years together. Jesus was
training these followers to be his ambassadors in the
world and authorizing them to fulfill his dream as
outlined in the Lord's Prayer: "Thy kingdom come, thy
will be done, on earth as it is in heaven." As I wrote
in *Dream Like Jesus*®, his vision was the earth would
somehow approximate heaven in its love, light, joy,
peace, forgiveness, humor, welcome, and equity.

These twelve disciples were a diverse group of people

who might not normally mix. Matthew, who cooperated with the Roman Empire by collecting exorbitant taxes, would have engendered a sense of betrayal among them. Simon, on the other hand, was associated with the zealots who aggressively fought Rome to protect Jewish national and religious concerns. The zealots were so intent on their agenda that they despised Jews who were conciliatory toward Rome. Can you imagine the fireworks when Matthew and Simon were in the same room? Yet these two, along with the other ten, transcended their differences to become trusted friends.

How? First, they embraced honesty and vulnerability, a willingness to be true to who they were and their life's experiences (the highs and lows, the good and the bad, the victories and the struggles) while challenging others in their life's journey and challenging themselves to grow. This level of transparency built trust, which must have been quite an undertaking for these twelve disciples who traveled with and learned from Jesus.

Life on the road with Jesus wasn't easy. Along the way, this group endured betrayal and a suicide as well as harassment from authorities, not to mention failure and doubt within. Several of the disciples thought about leaving Jesus. On more than one occasion, they didn't understand their leader or get where he was coming from. Despite all this, Jesus never kicked any of them out, nor did they leave. They felt safe enough to share what they really thought, felt, and believed. In other words, they practiced vulnerability, which then opened the door to accountability.

During their three years together, Jesus sent the Twelve (and others) on assignments where they were told to heal the sick, raise the dead, and share the coming and presence of God's Kin(g)dom. When the disciples completed their mission, they would return to Jesus to give account of who they spoke with and what they accomplished. There were also times when the Twelve saw failure in their work. Regardless of the outcome, the Twelve knew they were accountable to Jesus and loved by him.

Honesty, vulnerability, celebration, and accountability form an almost unbreakable foundation for spiritual community. When you look at your church, do you sense this level of connectedness? When people gather for worship, Sunday school, classes or small groups, during fellowship, or other events do they transparently disclose what's really going on with them? In the tough times, do they stick together to support each other? Do they share their struggles and overcome personal biases to be together? If we are to emulate Jesus' way, then we must build a true community within the church that is spiritual in nature rather than simply functional.

Virginia Greer, a clergy participant in Creating a Culture of Renewal®, recently moved cross-country to pastor a new church. Although she's long felt the love of God and claimed her place in the church, she still worried about not belonging. Her worries come partly from her fiancé's trans identity, but also from her own struggles with anxiety and depression. Even as a child she consciously worried about being "too much" for people. As she stepped into leadership in her new church, God's vision for Virginia and her community emerged: "building community where misfits fit." She longs for the church to be a place where all people, even the ones like herself, who feel like misfits, can join together in this journey of life, feeling connected and loved.

The Power of Being Social

Just as the shutdowns helped us reassess our relationship to work, they also showed us how much we value human interactions. Joni Mitchell famously sang, "You don't know what you've got til it's gone; they paved paradise and put up a parking lot." Even as we were shut in our homes, we quickly found our way online. Why? We are social beings; we need to be around other people. Even the greatest introvert suffers when they are isolated from others for too long.

You can see this intense need to be social in the way the coronavirus has played out over the last two years. As the first shutdowns of 2020 eased and people traveled over the Thanksgiving and Christmas holidays to hold new grandbabies, hug parents, and be in the company of others, it drove a second wave of COVID-19 infections.

By the time we hit spring and summer of 2021, the intense desire to be with others drove a third wave of COVID-19 infections powered by the delta variant. Having been separated for so long, people were eager to get together – to eat together, worship together, talk and laugh together. To be social. As of this writing, we are coming out of yet another wave of the pandemic, this time powered by the omicron variant.

The pandemic aside, when it comes to creating spiritual community, it's important to include a strong social element with many opportunities for social interaction. Looking at Jesus and his community of twelve is a case in point. As we've seen, they traveled together from one place to the next through challenging terrain on foot. Along the way, between the healings, the teachings, and providing provisions for large crowds, they got to know each other, discovered each other's strengths and weaknesses, and overcame political prejudices and regional biases, all of which gave them what they needed to stay together in the tough times. They also shared countless meals together, attended social gatherings, undertook fasts, celebrated feasts, and observed the festivals together. As disciples, they benefited from both the spiritual and social bonds in their lives.

I admit, "being social" sometimes gets a bad name in the church. Inward-focused church communities may be dismissed as little more than social clubs. Churches that focus less on being of service in the community than on hosting potlucks, socials, and meals for each other, can be seen as selfish or not really a church. In fact, I used to share that critical view: these weren't churches as much as they were social clubs.

But the pandemic has changed my mind. I now believe that the church, in addition to being spiritually-focused and service-oriented, needs to be a lot more socially minded. Here's my thinking. Social connections create a sense of belonging. A sense of belonging leads to emotional and relational stability and provides an ingredient essential to the formation of spiritual community: trust. Trust is built by the hard work of honesty, vulnerability, celebration, and accountability, as mentioned earlier. In addition to trust, belonging and stability are the blessed results of living in true community.

Ironically, I think there's a connection between the disconnect people feel in society and their disconnect from each other. Even before the pandemic, America was experiencing a crisis of connection, of belonging. Interestingly enough, according to a study of American life, this crisis of belonging isn't limited to a specific demographic or generation. The study shows that people of all demographics – including both Democrats and Republicans as well as the young and the elderly – experience a lack of connection with others. The shutdowns fueled the rise of mental health issues by forcing us apart even more than we already were. Longing to belong is as basic to human makeup as spirituality. In fact, satisfying the longing to belong is fundamental to creating a spiritual community.

Longing to Belong

A recent study conducted by neuroscientists at MIT, the Massachusetts Institute of Technology, found that cravings for human interactions and food register in the same part of the brain. Likewise, the pain of being excluded by others and physical pain are located in the same part of the brain. In other words, belonging is as delicious as your favorite food. Not belonging throbs like a broken bone.[37]

Belonging is a tricky thing, though. It doesn't always come from what you think might foster self-esteem, such as getting "likes" on social media. Social media platforms have, instead, trained people to observe and perform, seeking the endorphin surge of "likes." But those interactions ultimately make it harder to feel like you belong. Posting on social media is a poor replacement for live interactions with other human beings. "To truly feel a sense of belonging, you must feel unity and a common sense of character with and among members of your group," notes Tracy Brower in *Missing Your People: Why Belonging is So Important and How to Create It.*[38]

Belonging is a key aspect of mental health,

happiness, and productivity. This is especially true in a post-pandemic world. It's why creating true community at church – community that is both social and spiritual – is essential. Although one crucial element of belonging is having friends or being with like-minded people, there's more to belonging than that. Participating in groups is also important. The real power of belonging is activated when you are part of multiple groups: for instance, belonging to church, plus singing with the choir; or belonging to your family, plus being on the team that organizes the summer reunion; or belonging at work, plus being part of the group that plans the Christmas party. Or all of the above. The more groups you belong to – no matter how big or small – the more your self-esteem rises because it affirms that you belong. An enduring Harvard study revealed that "close relationships are what keep people happy throughout their lives, and these relationships with family, friends, and community delay mental and physical decline."[39] I assert that vibrant connections of belonging – to one another, to God, to the community at large – can delay organizational decline as well.

In a 2021 study, authors Brian Hardwick and Sebastian Buck asked people what creates these social connections or feelings of belonging. The most frequent answers they received included: "Everyone has a chance to have their voice heard" and "People can be who they want to be."[38] For a church to move from just offering church to building true community that's both social and spiritual entails creating multiple opportunities for people to belong. The shared identity that goes with belonging to a variety of groups – from a prayer group, to a covenant group, to a social group – boosts the immune system, wards off depression, and creates solidarity.

So what does it take to create true community at church that is both social and spiritual?

First, let's talk about what being social isn't. Being social isn't creating cliques that self-select for like-minded people. In other words, we're not talking about predominately white churches that close ranks against people of color. Or predominantly middle class churches that turn up their noses at those without a home. Or churches full of Boomers that don't want to change anything or appeal to younger generations. I'm not even talking about harmony-seeking churches that frown upon risk-takers or churches that turn their backs on the overly joyous or talkative.

Instead, when I talk about communities being social, I'm talking about churches that intentionally build bonds of connection between and among different kinds of people to form a sense of divine belonging, a sense of beloved community. The more people feel like they belong and that their contributions are welcome, the more they can risk the personal authenticity necessary to grow spiritually within the community.

Connect the Social and Spiritual

I arrived early for worship one morning and headed straight for the front chancel area since it was my turn to serve as liturgist. As soon as I arrived, I was invited to join the small choir that would be leading the singing. It was easy to say yes because I wouldn't have to worry about hitting every note; the pipe organ would be the dominant sound in the sanctuary. In between preparing the scripture reading, glancing at the call to worship, and scoping out the hymns on the order of worship, Linda, Dana, Susan, and I chatted about Linda's recent doctor's appointment, Susan's preparation for the children's sermon, and Dana's impeccable sense of timing. I'm not super close to these folks, but this kind of informal talk pulled us together as worship leaders and prepared us to enter into the spirit of worship by giving us a sense of belonging. I could feel the sense of connection deep in my bones.

At one level, being social is as simple as our informal visiting before worship. On another level, being social can be an even more intentional part of what it means to be spiritual. For instance, I noticed that as worship unfolded – since there was no passing of the peace or passing of offering plates – very few people moved or had speaking parts in the service. Along with the preacher and the musician, the small choir and I were responsible for all the service's active parts. That meant everyone else in worship was fairly passive. There wasn't even an official time to say hello to each other. This dynamic could be changed by asking people to exchange a few words with a person sitting nearby – like introducing yourself, sharing something you are grateful for, noting where God was present in the previous week, or exchanging a prayer concern. Those online could post something in the chat to share with others participating virtually. Even small social interchanges such as these can amplify a sense of belonging and create a greater sense of community.

Weaving the social and spiritual together can take place at a programmatic level by gathering folks together around common interests and needs. For example, find themes or activities that are biblical and contemporary with both social and spiritual aspects. Take cooking and eating, for example. They fit the bill. They're contemporary and biblical practices and have both social and spiritual aspects. Consider the meal Abram and Sarai made for the angelic visitors at the oaks of Mamre. Or the many times Jesus ate with others as occasions for fellowship and teaching. Or the post-resurrection meal Jesus shared with a handful of his disciples. In each instance, eating was both social and spiritual. Who doesn't know the transcendent experience of being nourished by just the right food at just the right time? Food is more than calories or nutrition. It provides the bridge for conversation and sustenance for the soul.

Resurrect the practice of building social and spiritual community around food by intentionally hosting classes or experiences that encompass these themes. For instance, in teaching people how to cook or garden, you could offer a store-to-plate or farm-to-table experience. As you first shop or garden, prepare, cook, and enjoy the food, you can interweave biblical themes like hospitality or care of the body into your discussions. Or, more simply, share a scripture or two. Then invite the Risen Christ to join you at the table. Not only will community form around these experiences, but these experiences themselves can lead to community-oriented projects or congregation-community partnerships.

When weaving together the social and the spiritual, the same sort of multi-faceted experience can apply to crafts and creativity, construction and building, parenting, and mentoring children or young adults. By designing gatherings that include both the social and spiritual, you promote spiritual and emotional growth while building community between and among members.

Youth and Young People

"As a dad, I blame myself," Ivan sighed. "It makes me very sad to see how all three of my kids are doing during the pandemic." Ivan is an effective pastor with a close family, but his three sons haven't fared that well during the last two years. Ivan's oldest son, who is twenty-six, zoned out for twenty minutes at choir practice. His friends couldn't even get his attention. Ivan's middle son is a twenty-two-year-old senior at the state university. When the choirs shut down, in-person practices and performances stopped. That cut out a big part of what brought him a sense of belonging. Now, his son won't even look at job opportunities, his way of avoiding future disappointment. Ivan's youngest son, seventeen years old, was continually quarantined because of close contact with his friends. Even though he wore a mask, he had been sent home from school two to three weeks at a time. "My kids are incredibly smart and talented in music," Ivan lamented. "But they look at the future, and they don't see themselves succeeding. It becomes a self-fulfilling prophecy."

Many young people like Ivan's kids experienced the devastation of an unknown or unseen future during the pandemic, which contributed to the mental health issues that teens and tweens already had to deal with. Their lack of social interaction and enforced isolation since 2020 has been especially hard on them. All people, but especially young people, thrive when they are part of a larger group. Maybe that's why Stephen's teenage stepdaughter reacted to the devastation of forced isolation by holding "Zoom happy hours" with her friends. "I don't know how prevalent alcohol use and abuse was for others," Stephen commented, "but it contributed to her decline during the shutdown."

It's not just young people who are dealing with mental health. Ivan's wife, an accomplished professional, was also "drowning in a sea of mental health issues" during the worst of the pandemic. She, too, struggled with depression and anxiety. Creating belonging is more essential than ever for us all.

As you set the stage for community that is both social and spiritual, remember that different generations long to belong in different ways. Don't expect people of different age groups to need or want the same things. Developmentally, Gen Z (born 1997-2009) and Generation Alpha (born 2010-present), for example, are in the stage of exploration. They're questioning, pushing the edges, and finding acceptance on their own terms. Give them space to ask questions and discover new answers. Moreover, Gen Z is among the most well-educated generation on the planet, as well as the most ethnically and racially diverse. Yet, Jeremy Adams, a California educator who wrote *Hollowed Out: A Warning About America's Next Generation,* calls these young people "a generation living solitary lives, hyper-connected to technology but unattached from their families, churches, or communities."[40]

While students might have been more connected to their families during the pandemic, with no live classes being held and little chance to be with classmates, their hyper-connectivity had to intensify. But, once schools opened up again, students who went against the norm and either wore or didn't wear masks experienced a different kind of social isolation. This social isolation at the hands of peers was especially hard on young people eager to reconnect with their friends.

Now is the perfect time to foster a new sense of belonging by intentionally connecting with young people on their terms. While not every young person expresses themselves this way, you should get used to tattoos, piercings, gender fluidity, a variety of hair styles and colors, and an ongoing quest for identity; cultivate a sense of wonder at the unique creativity they exhibit. Above all, practice love and refrain from judging. Judgmental criticism is one of the top reasons young people report for being uninterested in church.

Here's another opportunity for us to become like Jesus, who was and is always interested in people regardless of how they look, sound, think, or what their life experience has been.[41] Although it may feel easier to focus on adults at church while complaining that youth don't show up or contribute, stay intentional about discovering new ways to connect with young people. One way to do that is to shift your mindset from viewing youth and young adults as appendages to adults or families, to whole persons in their own right. Just as God meets them where they are, be encouraged to do the same.

As you refocus on young people, don't forget about the youngest of the young people. They are experiencing something most of us have never been through or could possibly understand. Their experiences of church have been shaped by what we never dreamed – days of closed doors. The challenge for adults – working remotely, periods of isolation, and limiting gatherings to just a few people – became everyday life for children. So, as your churches move forward, remember these children and their need to belong, feel safe, and experience stability.

Rev. Gerard Nsabimana, a participant in Creating a Culture of Renewal®, acknowledges that the presence of children in the church is often applauded and seen as a blessing of growth for the church. Gerard also notices, however, that the church frequently fails to draw children into the community and neglects an active role in their development.

One of the best ways to draw children and young people into spiritual community is by giving them a chance to talk about their own lives and do good things for others. Doing good for others not only fulfills the Golden Rule but also fuels endorphins, the feel-good chemicals of the brain. Additionally, it creates a network of safety and encourages love of God, neighbor, and self. Consider the "Greta Effect," named for Swedish teen Greta Thunberg who started Fridays for Future and organized climate strikes while in high school. She launched a worldwide movement of climate activism among young people who care deeply about the planet. Since then, she has been nominated for three Nobel Peace prizes.

The point is, don't underestimate young people. Instead, ask them what they are interested in and give them a chance to talk and be heard.

Sharing Sacred Space

"I'm a pastor, not a warehouse manager," said Leigh Goodrich to the church trustees when they complained that they had no free space to store things anymore. "I'm not here to deal with your stuff." The church was in the process of making space for a preschool, a new partner gained during the pandemic, when the complaint arose. Leigh remained unruffled. She encouraged them to continue clearing out the junk they had been storing for years. As the trustees cleared out the junk, they found they could welcome even more partners into the building.

"Because of two very strong partners that we have – an organization that helps with women's breast cancer survival and a preschool – we eventually balanced our budget. We were in the hole $35,000 to $45,000 a year, and we balanced that out during the pandemic because we were willing to share sacred space," Leigh explains.

The budget isn't the only thing that got balanced

out in this church. What started as a way of meeting financial troubles turned into a wholesale change in culture. This church now lives out its new value of sharing sacred space by partnering with organizations. Leigh reflected on the theological changes that undergird their commitment to spiritual community.

"One of the things that I've realized is that Jesus didn't walk around going, 'Oh, I'm so poor. I don't have any money. I gotta live in a deficit budget. What am I going to do?' No. Jesus walked around looking for opportunities to help other people. If you're the body of Christ, you need to be free enough to do that, and part of that freedom is using your facility wisely."

The Power of Community to Heal

We are living in a time of deep political, economic, religious, social, racial, and generational polarization. This polarization is undergirded by what Arthur Brooks calls the "culture of contempt." In the culture of contempt, differences are framed as fatal, which deepens distrust of the other and encourages a gleeful sense of superiority over others. Most of all, this culture of contempt fuels an ever-ready sense of outrage, draining us before we even get to the issues that ought to cause real outrage: human trafficking, homelessness, hunger, poverty, and hierarchies based on color, money, or privilege.

In the culture of contempt, families are at odds, marriages are broken up, and longstanding friendships are ruined. Even congregations are torn apart. "In the past decade, we've watched a trickle in the decline of church membership turn to a geyser as people woke up to the incompatibility between the teachings of Jesus Christ and the practices of many who claim to follow him," writes Rev. Melissa Florer-Bixler. She notes the ripple effect:

> *Until recently, I was certain the death of the institutional church would come because of a mass exodus from the pews. But if the data is any indicator, the sun might set on U.S. churches as we know them because pastors refuse to aid and abet a compromise between factionalism and the good news of Jesus.*[35]

Can we deal with polarization and the culture of contempt using the gift of spiritual community? Rev. Derek Kubilus suggests an innovative way to address deep differences in the church. "Debate only drives it deeper," he cautions. "Ridicule only exacerbates the problem." To address these challenges, Derek suggests using a form of engagement called "motivational interviewing" in which a person asks three questions of another person:

- Why do you believe what you believe?

- What led you to these ideas?

- What makes these ideas so convincing for you?

For conversations like this to work, however, he says it's necessary to "create a safe space where folks can feel free to interrogate their [own] beliefs under an umbrella of trust, transparency, and vulnerability." As we've seen, spiritual community can create this sort of safe space. "While arguing and debating another's point of view drive us deeper into our trenches, sharing stories can bring sunlight to our wounds." Derek notes, "It's only in telling it that they can hear how ridiculous it sounds."[42] While Derek suggests this process for de-escalating and re-integrating conspiracy theorists into the life of the church, I think motivational interviewing can work for any kind of polarization. Because it does not dehumanize the other, rather, it deepens a sense of belonging by creating curiosity and connection.

In order to forge a new path and move the church forward in a post-pandemic world, it's time to reclaim the art of talking and listening to each other. Spiritual community, deeply founded in the love and grace of God, provides the necessary framework for this kind of risky, vulnerable conversation. To sustain us in community-building, I suggest also practicing the Platinum Rule.

Practice the Platinum Rule

Jesus counsels us through the Golden Rule to treat others in the way we ourselves would like to be treated. If you don't want to be lied to, don't lie to others. If you want to be treated with respect, respect others. The

Platinum Rule builds on the Golden Rule, and takes it one step further. The Platinum Rule suggests that we honor the dignity of those who are different, sometimes very different, from us, by treating them the way they want to be treated. For instance, my friend Cherisa wants to be referred to as Black, while David prefers African American. Nyx prefers the personal pronoun "they" instead of "he" or "she." My husband Jerry prefers to be identified as Hispanic or Latino, but definitely not Latinx. How do you keep all this straight? When in doubt, ask! Applying the Platinum Rule requires getting to know people in your community, asking questions, and finding out how they want to be treated.

The Platinum Rule not only applies to those with different beliefs, backgrounds or lifestyles than us, it applies to people whose personalities differ as well. Instead of rolling your eyes at the person who analyzes every risk, or insists on making friends with every stranger, or takes command to get things moving, or refuses to take the next step until every person has been heard – let go of judgment. Instead, honor their behavior as an expression of their unique humanity.

Practicing the Platinum Rule isn't always easy. It requires a hidden superpower: the ability to be a non-anxious presence. Everyone feels anxiety to some degree about certain things. But noticing your own tendency to be anxious helps you not project that on other people. This superpower is not as thrilling as being invisible like the Invisible Woman, or stretchy like Mister Fantastic, or able to leap over tall buildings in a single bound like Superman. However, this superpower is exceedingly useful for disciples and apostles of Jesus, people who care about Jesus' dream: "Thy kingdom come, thy will be done, on earth as it is in heaven."

The ability to be a non-anxious presence comes from letting go of ego and the need to be "right." It comes from giving up the need to prove another "wrong." You gain the capacity to be comfortable with just about anybody. Without blaming or judging them, or alternatively, being victimized by them.

To effectively use the Platinum Rule, remember three basic rules of emotional intelligence. First, ascribe good motives to others. Give people the benefit of the doubt. Trust that God loves them as much as God loves you – even if you disagree wildly on other matters. Second, strive to understand the situation from another's point of view. At the same time, don't drop your own values or perspective. Simply expand your capacity to acknowledge theirs too. Third, embrace differences; don't eliminate them.

As you practice the Platinum Rule, you will find yourself becoming more self-regulated. This self-regulation gives others permission to calm themselves. Calm thinking and deep faith allow all of you to tap into creativity and collaboration instead of contempt or grievance. As you model this, others can rise to the occasion and join you in practicing the Platinum Rule.

Tips for Building True Community

When it comes to building community, here are five tips:

Start Small Groups

Small groups have always been at the heart of the church. Jesus conducted the first small groups as he called disciples and then sent them out as apostles. His small group lasted a mere three years, but all of his students became teachers of new classes after he died and was resurrected.

Many churches are creatively reinvigorating their outreach by crafting "fresh expressions" of faith, including initiatives like Pub Theology or Bibles and Beer. Instead of insisting that new people come to the church to worship with them, church folks meet people at bars, pubs, coffee shops, laundromats, and restaurants to engage in faith discussion with them. Sometimes informal settings outside the church encourage greater self-revelation and an easier way to get to know each other.

Keep it Short and Sweet

Spend time together but keep your offerings short and sweet. People's attention spans have shortened, and their lives have gotten busier. Instead of a year-long Bible study, offer a four-to-six-week study. Instead of a ninety-minute learning session, try forty-five-minutes instead. Instead of a three-day retreat, invite others to a three-hour retreat. The point is to build togetherness with the time that people have. Many touches with the same people over time will build a more enduring community than one long experience never to be replicated.

Mix Social and Spiritual

Intentionally combine the social and the spiritual to create stronger community. Often small groups are organized around spiritual material, and the social part gets added in. But I want to encourage you to think about having groups based on social activities that add in the spiritual. For instance, gather a group that enjoys going to the movies, with a meal before or after the film. Discuss religious or spiritual themes in the movie, letting the movie prompt discussion about your own lives. End your time together by praying for one another.

Start with an Existing Community

Pastor RJ Davis noted that the congregation he serves was founded out of a housing development. These neighbors already had strong relationships and realized they wanted to be able to worship together, so they contacted denominational authorities and asked for a church to be planted there. True to their community nature, this congregation is all about doing life together. "People go to dinner together, take vacations together, and celebrate their kids' birthdays together," RJ notes. Others want to be part of this level of community, and it's brought new people to the church. Their new vision is to "Bring intentional community back to the neighborhood."

Do it Together

Remember that no one person can do this work alone. As the church comes together as community, approach community-building as Rev. Heather Bailes Baker learned to do. At first, Heather went about her work in the church, fearing she was burdening others when asking them to help or lead ministries. This fear left her shouldering too many responsibilities for rebuilding and growing the church. As she learned to delegate responsibilities to others, she saw a new way to approach the work ahead, referring to it as "our" work, not simply her work as the clergy. Building community is always "our" work.

Our Identity in Christ

When we are "in church," we come together as a group of people. We typically greet one another, join our voices together in song and prayer, hear the preached Word, and offer some kind of response. Our hearts are warmed at seeing folks we may not have seen in the past week and to catch up on the most recent sports event, what's happening in the community, or recent news, good or bad, that has rocked our state, nation, or world. After church, we may join others for lunch, then prepare to return to the church at the next appointed time, whether that be a mid-week Bible study, committee meeting, church project, or worship the following Sunday. Most likely, we love our church.

It's one thing to be "in church." It's quite different to be "in community." When we are in community, our care and love for one another go deeper than singing together and catching up on the latest news. Our care and love for others dares go to the soul, where the question shifts from "What's new?" to "How is it with your soul?"

When you move from being "in church" to being "in community," your vision of others changes. You glimpse Jesus in the eyes of the person next to you. You sense the Spirit in the questions from the new person. You look for opportunities to heal relationships instead of avoid conflict, or to address issues instead of let them fester. Judgments about others fall away as you practice the Platinum Rule. The temptation to gossip is replaced by the desire to get to know new people. Our defenses fall as we seek to find our identity in Christ and in Christian community. Imagine church as a place where people can share the depths of their lives without fear of gossip or rejection. Where the values of honesty, vulnerability, celebration, and accountability hold sway, and where we know that God speaks to us – and invites – our response.

CHAPTER SIX

Adopt the Culture of Technology to Do More with Less

Tech Revolutions Then and Now

During the pandemic, Zoom and other online technologies changed how we interacted with one another. Interestingly, this pandemic-inspired push toward online adoption has impacted not only congregations, but schools, nonprofits, businesses large and small, mental health providers, and doctors. The whole world is making this leap.[43]

Just as the COVID-19 pandemic created this surprising tech advance, so the bubonic plague created its own tech advances, ones we take for granted today. From the refinement of the printing press, to the mass production of books, to the rapid spread of information, to the active collaboration of a wide range of voices in science and the arts – all of this got its start during the bubonic plague.

Before the advent of Gutenberg's printing press around 1450, scribes painstakingly copied books by hand onto parchment and vellum made from animal skins. The plague created at least five new conditions.

First, the large number of people who died led to an abundance of clothing that was no longer needed. This clothing surplus created a new, abundant source of material for printing that was much less expensive than animal skins. Second, the monks who transcribed the Bible by hand were among those who died. With the marked decrease in scribes, the need for alternate ways to print materials was greater than ever. Third, the redistribution of wealth and the rise of the middle class meant more people could afford to buy books, which were quite expensive. Literacy grew as well. Fourth, information could be accurately copied and distributed quickly, creating a way for new voices and competing ideas to be heard. Before the printing press, you could burn a heretic at the stake and rid the world of their unwanted ideas once and for all. But once the written word could be copied and quickly distributed, new ideas could survive and persist.

The technological advancement of the printing press led to Martin Luther becoming the first best-selling author. Luther's *Ninety-five Theses* was copied onto broadsheet and distributed a mere seventeen days later. Luther, speaking to the role of the printing press in the Protestant Reformation, exulted, "Printing is the ultimate gift of God and the greatest one."[44] Paradoxically, one of Gutenberg's printing projects was producing indulgences for the Catholic Church, the very thing that Luther protested. But Gutenberg also printed almost 200 copies of the Bible in Latin. This project took almost three years, a mere blink of an eye compared to copying the Bible by hand. Gutenberg's Bible led to Luther's Bible, which was translated into German. As the printing press made books more widely available in a variety of languages, ideas spread quickly, transforming theology and science from solitary endeavors into communal endeavors as practitioners contributed to a body of common, shared knowledge.

After the plague was finally over, people did not look back and say, "Thank goodness we can be done with books now, or Protestantism, or the study of science." Rather, people who had a book in their hand for the first time looked forward to the future. They felt excitement and wonder as affordable books came into being. Knowledge is power.

The fact that you have Bibles on your shelf or in hand in a language you can understand is due to the post-plague tech revolution. And in our fast-paced, modern society, just when we think innovative technologies have reached their end, another gadget, platform, software, or smartphone hits the market. As a result, children can learn with their teacher and classmates while sitting at home. Education continues to evolve with students carrying fewer books to school, if any, and getting instant feedback from their teachers.

In the church, meetings, Bible study, worship, and even communion can be held online. Even folks who don't like to drive at night, have an opportunity to be involved. Families with a sick child can attend worship and comfort their child at the same time. Growth in technology has forever changed our expectations about what's possible. As this pandemic ends, I doubt we will say, "Thank goodness! Now we don't have to meet online anymore. We'll happily drive two hours for a one hour meeting."

Online Is Here to Stay

If you had people tuning in to your worship from across the country and even other parts of the world, did you shut it down with the reintroduction of in-person worship? Probably not. Patrick McPherson told me, "Every Sunday, I've got people tuning in from New Jersey, Florida, Texas, California, Arizona. I don't think it's a pandemic thing. I think this is the future. The church is facing the next Reformation."

While the pandemic has hastened online adoption in almost every area of our lives, it was only a matter of time before the church had to wrestle with it too. To truly thrive, the church must think about how to continue adapting and doing ministry in all forms online, especially with all generations. That doesn't mean we give up in-person experiences. However, it does mean we incorporate virtual options and offerings. As

Patrick McPherson noted, probably 40 to 50 percent of United Methodist churches in Oklahoma were strictly off-line before the pandemic. Like many other areas of the country, churches and people had to quickly move online. The question is, now that you're there, how will you stay and continue to adapt?

Digital technology is the new reformation. Like books expanded the reach of knowledge post-plague, online offerings erase distance, connect communities, and give instant access to new people and places post-pandemic. My friend and colleague, Rev. Charlotte Pridgen Randolph, discovered this for her New England congregation. She recalled, "When COVID-19 hit, our first worship was done using telephone conferencing. The reception was horrible. Week two, we were using a free Zoom account and the time ran out on us. I was horrified, but the church was gracious. By week three, we had ordered a camera, signed up for a paid Zoom account, and we were on our way." She continued, admitting, "I was apprehensive about the technology, but I realized that through the unplanned changes, technology allowed me to reach people on both coasts and around New England. Our church now provides hybrid worship and we still have people from both the east and west coasts joining us."

While the pandemic pushed us toward adopting digital technology, it wasn't simply a fluke. Digital technology is now essential to moving forward into the future. The world has come to expect it. Once people have online options, they treasure them. Online worship means your people can participate while traveling, indisposed, sick, or pressed for time. Don't give any of that up, even though face-to-face worship is once again available. In this way, you can continue to maintain and even expand your reach and mission. Online options also help you extend your shelf life. Unlike starting an additional worship service, which depends on a certain number of people in attendance to be considered viable, online worship lives in a different time frame. It can be experienced hours or months later and still be fresh – especially as you incorporate the culture shifts of spirituality and community.

As with any new technology, people and institutions adopt them at different rates. Thom Rainer identifies three categories of adoption: digital-only, digitally transitioning, and dual citizens. As Sarah Payne pointed out: "You can't master technology because it's always changing." However, staying on the journey of adopting technology is essential.

Your congregation is important to your community. Your message is more relevant than ever before. Embracing technology, without breaking the bank or overloading your people, is important. With the whole world moving online, your church needn't be left behind.

The Benefits of Hybrid Worship

If you and your congregation find yourself with a sharp decrease in worship attendance, you will be interested to learn that not all churches do. According to the Hartford Institute for Religion Research, which surveyed 2,074 churches from a cross-section of thirty-eight denominations in the summer of 2021, 28 percent of congregations actually grew over the past two years. Of that percentage, 18 percent of those congregations reported a startling growth of 25 percent or more. That's pretty astonishing in the middle of a pandemic.

How could some churches experience such growth and others not? What made the difference?

Here's the scoop. Whether a church experienced an increase or decrease in worship attendance had to do with whether or not they ventured into hybrid worship. Congregations that stuck with in-person worship only (15 percent of the surveyed group) experienced the sharpest decline in worship attendance by more than 15 percent. On the other hand, congregations that offered only online worship also declined. However, their decline was at a lower rate of just over 7 percent.

Growth in worship attendance came with congregations that offered a hybrid experience of worship – that is simultaneous in-person and online worship. Those congregations grew by 4.5 percent during the last two years. While that's not a huge number, it's distinctly different from the losses of 7 to 15 percent of those who didn't. It's not that these hybrid-worshiping congregations did everything right or felt completely comfortable and equipped to do things differently. In fact, they reported that they, too, struggled to change and adapt. But because they moved forward anyway, they saw a benefit. For them, the cameras represented their community and their mission field.

When you think about hybrid worship, consider that it doesn't have to be limited to live-streaming worship combined with some in-person worship. Instead, think about creating online resources that people can access in their daily lives. In this way, worship becomes a way of life, not just a Sunday morning experience. As you give your congregation tools to experience God all week long, you have made the most of technology. For instance, Pastor Kris Mayberry records eight-minute podcasts of prayer. Her messages are brief and effective. These crisp, clear, and concise recordings are easily available and can be accessed in the garden, during a workout, while driving, or at the dinner table.

Generations and Tech

Even as technology is here to stay, the way different generations do tech varies. For instance, while Boomers were raised on TV, Gen Z's are digital natives born with cell phones in their hands. They approach technology completely differently. Take the YouTube twin sensation, Tim and Fred Williams, born in 1998. These twenty-somethings from Gary, Indiana, were raised on Christian rap and gospel music in church. Now, they post video reactions of themselves listening to other styles of music for the first time.

Their reaction videos have ranged from Queen's "Bohemian Rhapsody" to Whitney Houston's "I Will Always Love You" to Michael Jackson's tight and precise moonwalking. So popular are these Gen Z'ers that their videos have gone viral, causing Boomer Phil Collins's 1981 song, "Something in the Air Tonight," to hit #2 on iTunes, almost forty years after its release. Their reaction to Dolly Parton's "Jolene" got such a response that Saturday Night Live, the enduring comedy show of the Boomers, picked it up and did a sketch on the twins. But the twins had not even heard of *Saturday Night Live.* What did they do? They posted a reaction video after hearing about *Saturday Night Live* for the first time. They have 884,000 subscribers to their Twinsthenewtrend YouTube channel and have made over 1,400 videos. They have the impact equivalent to a mega-mega church. What makes them so attractive? It's the experience and genuineness that trend-hunter Jeremy Gutsche described.

The Williams brothers are so open to different kinds of music and so authentic that you feel right there with them as they watch and react to the music. Do you know who loves these videos? You got it. Boomers. They love

137

watching their music being appreciated by a whole new generation. What if your young people were to make reaction videos to elements of church life, sacraments, hymns, or biblical stories? Or just life in general? What kind of impacts might that create?

Tips for Technology

Consider these words from Upper Room's master innnovator Terrell L McTyer, "The cousin of relevance is audience." Keep your audience in mind as you choose which technologies to incorporate. Select ones that will be relevant and accessible for your particular congregation and community. When it comes to smaller or older congregations, avoid the mistake of doing too much too fast. Smaller and older churches tend to be late adopters. They won't be the first on the technology bandwagon, but they needn't be the last. If you do too much too fast, you'll hit a wall of resistance. Instead, start with what is most needed and go from there.

I suggest you follow these three steps for small churches to embrace technology.

Step One: Get Up to Date

The first step in embracing technology is to make sure your basic tech is working and functional. For instance, does your small church have a working phone with voicemail and an up-to-date phone message? Does the congregation own and use a computer? Is email set up?

In August of 1999, when I arrived to pastor the Rawlins, Wyoming congregation I mentioned earlier, I found that the church was off the grid. The photocopier was on the fritz, the voicemail was disabled, the computer was iffy, and they had no email account. Within the first month of my tenure, I ensured the basic technology was up and working. By the time December 31, 1999, came around, we were online enough to be worried by the Y2K scare. Several years later, the congregation was gifted a screen and overhead projection system. I was concerned that the older generation wouldn't like it, but they surprised me. They loved how large the words were, and the enhanced visibility made singing louder and easier.

When it comes to technology, start with the basics before you expand. And I mean basics: a telephone, a printer or photocopier, a computer, and an email account. For many congregations, the basics also include an overhead projection system. Of course, if you don't have indoor plumbing or electricity, you might want to start there!

Step Two: Get Connected to the Outside World

The second step in embracing technology is to get connected to the outside world. After you've got the basics, expand to include a Facebook page or a website. If you don't have your own website, make sure your congregation is noted on regional or denominational

FORGING A NEW PATH

websites with correct worship times and days, address (both physical and digital), and pastor or congregational leader.

By the time I left that beloved Wyoming congregation some seven years later, the congregation also had a working website. Although Facebook didn't exist at the time, when it came into being, someone saw to it that a Facebook page was established.

Step Three: Hybrid Worship

The third step is to make the move to bring your worship online. Keep it simple by using a smartphone and a tripod to live-stream your worship on Facebook. During worship, be sure to address the people who are watching, worshiping, and participating with you online. Even if they watch later, they are still part of your congregation. Be sure to welcome and include them in the message, the prayers, and the offering. Likely you'll find your worship attendance growing as you intentionally acknowledge your online audience.

Step Four: Online Giving

If your congregation currently relies on older givers to sustain the finances of the church, educate all your people to adopt the subscriber mode of giving. Moving from the pay-per-view approach to online subscribership means the church also has to be worth investing in and supporting sacrificially. Just as people pay for gym

140

memberships even when they don't go because of the promise it provides, people need to have a positive vision of what the church provides them and the community before investing proactively.

I think it's important and helpful to shift our thinking from "I tithe because it's the right thing to do and my religious duty" (which has a distinctly Pioneer generation ethos to it) to "I invest in this congregation because of what's in it for me and others," which taps into the Boomer and Millennial ethos. What's in it for "me" isn't necessarily about what a person "gets" from church, although that's part of it. It's also the benefit a person gets from living in a community that is strengthened by a vibrant church that meets needs and provides value to so many. Again, your church then needs to provide that value to its members and its community. Likely you're already doing so, but you may not be used to framing giving in this way.

Another benefit to online giving is that it allows people in your community to contribute directly to the church. When people spot your congregation doing good, they want to be able to honor that. Giving the community a way to contribute is very important. It also allows you to understand that you are a community asset. The times an offering plate has been absent from occasional services has always troubled me. I want to give and to bless. The communities we serve feel the same way. They may not come to the building to put a check in the plate, but they'd love to find a way to say thank you. Make it easy. This is an important pivot for the church: to not only say that we are here to make a difference in our communities but allow the community to say thank you in an easy, accessible, touch-free way.

The Hartford Institute for Religion Research reports that increases in giving outweighed decline in giving in the second year of the pandemic. While 30 percent of the cross-section of churches surveyed reported a decline in giving, 40 percent reported the opposite. Their giving actually increased. Thirty percent of churches reported that giving stayed steady.

Small Church Technology Do's and Dont's

Do make progress. You can go farther than you think you can. By incorporating technology and accepting the learning curve that comes with it, you may be surprised how quickly you learn how to use the tools that are most helpful and necessary for your congregation.

Do use the technology you invest in for multiple purposes. A webcam is a great tool that can be used to record, live-stream, or take worship to Zoom. This will allow greater participation for members who aren't comfortable returning to church or can't attend in person every week. It can also be used for hosting online and hybrid meetings, Bible studies, and impromptu messages throughout the week.

Do think of embracing technology as a journey, not an event. Technology isn't going away. You can't master it. None of us can. But you also don't have to resist the flow of it.

Don't assume that older people do not want to embrace technology. Many of them join kids and grandkids on weekly Zoom meetings, FaceTime visits, and the like. Also, don't assume that every young person is constantly on their smartphone or even has a smartphone.

Don't make tech decisions based solely on cost. Money that goes toward getting or upgrading outdated technology is money well spent. The benefits of buying quality equipment that will allow you to reach a larger community are unmatched.

Don't do it by yourself. Look for people in your congregation or larger community who can help you. They're out there, and they are often quite happy to share their knowledge. At the very least, remember you can Google any question and watch YouTube videos on almost any subject.

When it comes to technology, the point isn't to be trendy. Rather, it's to find new ways to connect. Just as the Bible reminds us that even feet can be beautiful as they carry the good news, so, too, can new technologies. They enable us to carry good news in fresh ways.

The Culture of Digital Technology

While online tech is the answer for many congregations, not every church will be able to do all the things they'd like to do. So what if you can't do it all or you just don't have the people who can do tech?

Technology itself is not a utopian solution. It's more about the culture that digital technology has brought about. Ryan Panzer, author of *Grace and Gigabytes,* concedes that it's not so much that churches need to become masters of technology. There are endless opportunities that simply can't be mastered. Rather than try to stay abreast of every platform, keep up with every breaking trend, and use every app, he suggests that you look instead to the culture that digital technology has created. He calls this "tech-shaped culture." Its four values include questions, connection, collaboration, and creativity.

Let's look at them in turn.

Questions: Invitation to New Answers

Long before she had ALS, my mother was the first person I heard say, "Let me Google it," when looking for an answer to a question. Now "Google" is an accepted verb and a commonplace way of researching information on the internet. Practically everybody uses it.

The ability to ask a question and have Alexa, Siri, or Google answer your question is a turning point in the quest for knowledge. Before these search engines, knowledge was organized by answers, not by questions. If you wanted to know what dinosaurs ate, you had to find a specialized book, or look up the entry "dinosaurs" in an encyclopedia, then browse the entire book or article to pick up the answer to the question. That's very different from asking, "Siri, what did dinosaurs eat?" Further, encyclopedia entries are contained, assuming this information is all we know, or maybe even this is all there is to know about any particular field of study.

A question-oriented culture is a major shift in context. Asking questions pushes boundaries and opens possibilities. The question-asking culture encourages curiosity, agency, and engagement. It assumes that no question is off-limits, that every question has an answer, that a range of answers is available, and that questions are good and welcome.

In church cultures where every correct answer is "Jesus," this sort of open-endedness and freedom can be both uncomfortable and exhilarating. It expands the boundaries of what can be created. So how can you encourage the asking of questions? Start by being willing to entertain and engage questions. Ask open-ended questions during worship and Bible study rather than give answers. Allow new points of view to shape new answers – especially points of view that come from a variety of generations and backgrounds. Allow people time to process, ask new questions, and discern the best answers.

Connection: Transcending Boundaries

The second value of the tech-shaped culture is connection. Digital technology connects people in Zoom rooms, on FaceTime, and through Facebook Live. It even connects people across the physical and the virtual, creating hybrid experiences. It transcends boundaries like location and distance in real-time, allowing for connection across many realms.

Collaboration: Participation and Contribution

In addition to online platforms like Zoom that allow people to meet together in real-time, other online tools allow people to collaborate by creating documents. Google Docs is one prime example. The world has come to expect collaboration, Google Docs has made it easier. Working together makes for stronger buy-in. It includes many points of view, and it engenders a sense of community. Leadership in the church is often seen as top-down, or sometimes, bottom-up. But imagine collaborating laterally in the realms of worship, mission, liturgy, and the future of the church. This type of teamwork goes beyond committee planning to a deeper give-and-take between and among people. Collaboration is consistent with our trinitarian theology. Just as the three persons of the trinity flow into one another and become inseparable, so collaboration produces something that is greater than the sum of it's parts.

Creativity: An Expression of the Divine Within

In the online world, each person is a content creator. From the simplest post to sharing photographs to recording a video, social media platforms have encouraged an explosion of creativity. This profusion of self-expression can easily be encouraged and included in the church as well. Imagine people sharing their prayers, artwork, and unique spiritual experiences with one another. Historically, church has been a venue for creativity from spoken word, to fabric arts, liturgical dance, and music ranging from classical to traditional to innovative. Creativity is the ultimate expression of the divine Creator. As we share our own creativity, we have the opportunity to expand the presence of God in the world.

In Ryan Panzer's article, "Digital Ministry: More about Culture than Computers," he keeps technology in proper perspective by focusing attention on what tech can do for Christianity. "We don't need to be sophisticated users of technology; sometimes we may not need much technology at all," says Ryan. "As church leaders, we simply need to notice these values in action and to determine how they align to God's work in our Christian community."[45]

Church in the Round

Making this shift to a tech-shaped culture doesn't require any special equipment. All it requires is a change in focus. When you think about it, church sanctuaries are arranged like classrooms of old where a teacher stood in front of the class to dispense knowledge. But even classrooms have changed. Instead of a teacher standing in front of rows of desks, children are often arranged in huddles of desks so that students can learn together in groups. Students not only learn from the teacher, but they also learn from each other and from other sources such as books, online resources, and outside experts. One way this recent model of learning can be applied to the church is to envision church in the round.

Open Space is one such example. This format, developed by Rev. Mary Beth Taylor, forms Jesus-based community by fostering open-ended questions and discussion about matters of faith during in-person and online church meetings. Mary Beth has found particular success with bringing young people in by offering permission to ask questions in a safe and welcoming space. When churches discourage questions, they self-sabotage by pushing younger generations away, making them feel as though they should just "be quiet and believe everything they're told."[46] Only, that's not the way it works anymore. Not in a tech-shaped culture. In a tech-shaped culture, questions, connections, creativity, and collaboration means anyone and everyone can participate.

Our Identity in Christ

I've already shared that deepening our spirituality will shift us from knowing about our identity in Christ to experiencing our identity in Christ, thereby strengthening our relationship with Christ. As we live into our spirituality and come together in genuine spiritual community, this journey called life is no longer my life to live; it's our life to live – a group effort. In spiritual community that honors honesty, vulnerability, celebration, and accountability, you always have someone you can share the depths of your heart and soul with and not fear being in tomorrow's gossip chain. You see in each other the heartbeat of Jesus and a life that models God's love.

As children of God, made in the image of God, and having our identity in Christ, we hold within us traits of God, including the power to create. Creativity, in one form or another, is part of our DNA. You may say, "I don't have a creative bone in my body," but you don't have to sculpt like Michelangelo, write hymns like Charles Wesley, sing like Lady Gaga, or write and produce movies like Tyler Perry to be creative. Creativity can be innovative thinking or the ability to look at what you have and make something miraculous. It can be posting a great meme or collaborating on a new ministry or even asking a new question.

Let your identity in Christ be your guide as you adopt

the culture of technology in your church. Remember that, with adoption, the future is unknown or unclear. It takes a leap of faith to choose a new path, to choose something you've never done before. Look past the barriers of "We've never done it this way before" to what's possible when you approach the future from your identity in Christ.

Tech has expanded our sense of incarnation. No longer limited to the physical, we have extended ourselves into the virtual. In much the same way that God stretched from the invisible to the visible through Christ, we are extending beyond the tangible into the intangible through digital connections.

CHAPTER SEVEN

Living Out the Mission of the Post-Pandemic Church

At the end of the Gospel of Matthew, Jesus gives the newly formed church their marching orders. Known as the Great Commission (Matthew 28:16-20), these words have guided the church for centuries:

> *Then the eleven disciples went to Galilee, to the mountain where Jesus had told them to go. When they saw him, they worshiped him; but some doubted. Then Jesus came to them and said, "All authority in heaven and on earth has been given to me. Therefore go and make disciples of all nations, baptizing them in the name of the Father and of the Son and of the Holy Spirit, and teaching them to obey everything I have commanded you. And surely I am with you always, to the very end of the age."*

These words continue guiding the church today. You could say this commission has defined the mission of the church from its earliest expansion through the many chapters of church life, even up to and through the pandemic. Our work is to bring others into the life of discipleship, follow the teachings of Jesus, and launch ourselves into apostolic work as well.

However, considering the pandemic and all the changes it has brought, the way we interpret and apply the Great Commission needs to change. Throughout this book, I've shown that to forge a new path and move the church forward in a post-pandemic world, it's time to courageously implement three key shifts in culture: embrace spirituality as the next normal, invite people back to church as community, and adopt the culture of technology to do more with less.

How do we live out the mission of the post-pandemic church with these shifts in place?

First, the COVID-19 pandemic forced churches to see beyond their own walls to other "pandemics" impacting the communities around them. This awakening sharpened consciousness about food insecurity, racial injustice, and the vulnerability of front-line workers. It also prompted churches to align with their communities in new ways. During 9/11, we focused our gratitude on firefighters and first responders. Two decades later, our attention and compassion grew to include health care workers, restaurant workers, sanitation workers, and others whose work was deemed not only essential, but vital to our ability to get through the pandemic somewhat intact as a society. We responded to the rising tide of White nationalism and White supremacy as we bore witness to the terror of Asian scapegoating and the stark injustices against the African American community.

In light of these many pandemics, there are new

how's and why's for deepening the spiritual growth and influence of the church.

No Need to Fear Change

Pastor and teacher Alex Shea Will notes, "The urgency of the pandemic freed us collectively from the fear of change. Many of my colleagues and I found our congregations looking to us for adaptation. The moment forced us not only to talk about change but to enact it."[47]

The pandemic freed us, rather unceremoniously, of mindsets that hampered church growth for years and years. Many of these shifts, decades in the making, swept obstacles away seemingly overnight. The good news is the church has already made three profound changes in attitude that move the church forward.

The first change in attitude had us go from saying, "We've never done it that way before" to "Whatever it takes to stay together." Before the pandemic, invoking the seven last words of the church, "We've never done it that way before," derailed many needed changes in congregational life. Uttering those seven words was a sign that tradition had again triumphed over risk. With the rapid onset of the coronavirus and the changes it necessitated, congregations quickly became aware that this first pre-pandemic mindset wouldn't do. To continue resisting change would mean nothing less than abandoning the church.

As church doors slammed shut to slow contagion, congregations adopted practices they had resisted for years. For instance, most congregations never dreamed they would launch Facebook Lives or online worship services in a matter of days. Yet fueled by a desire to maintain the church body, congregations adopted a new mindset, saying, "We'll do whatever it takes to stay together." This first change in attitude bore surprising fruit. Many congregations quickly moved online to offer prayer, Bible Study, worship, and fellowship.

The second change in attitude had us go from saying, "The church is the building" to "We are the church." Before the pandemic, churches were almost strictly building-based. In many ways, the care and maintenance of buildings was the shadow mission of many churches. In the process of living into the new reality of shutdowns, to be the church, it became apparent that churches didn't need their buildings – no matter how sacred. While a familiar hymn long proclaimed, "The church is not a building, the church is not a steeple, the church is not a resting place, the church is a people," it was a relatively untried theory until March 2020.

While Christians believe that out of death comes resurrection, even the most faithful would've been hard-pressed to envision the new life for congregations that arose out of the shutdowns. Worshipers and worship leaders were set loose from decades of doing things just so.

The third change in attitude had us go from saying, "Wait and see" to "Ownership and agency." Before the pandemic, many churches were in wait-and-see mode, as in, "Let's wait and see what General Conference decides, then we'll know what we are supposed to do." This reactive approach has had a disastrous impact on morale, ministry, and mission. As long as you are waiting for "them" to tell you what to do or who you are, you deflect your own agency and become a stumbling block for the Kin(g)dom. The wait-and-see approach is also used between appointments. "Let's wait and see what the new pastor or the new bishop wants to do here." But wait-and-see means God can no longer move through you. Your congregation is effectively off-limits for God's work. Over the years, the wait-and-see mindset has squandered momentum, delayed dreams, and stalled partnerships. It has meant justice delayed – and justice denied.

Through the pandemic, many congregations shrugged off the wait-and-see mode as they dared to step into the immediacy of the moment. Whether organizing for racial justice, offering respite to essential front-line workers, or ministering to those orphaned by COVID-19, churches sprang into action to offer on-the-spot ministry to those in need. This new sense of ownership meant that church buildings quickly transformed into vaccination sites, overnight homeless shelters, and pop-up food banks.

The Next Good Crisis

COVID-19 has forever disrupted the notion that churches can't flex and adapt. Churches used the current crisis well by demonstrating increased adaptability, resilience, and creativity. As churches rose brilliantly to the occasion, dire circumstances were no match for the faith-based community. They quickly moved online, distinguished between owning a building and being the church, and expanded their sense of ownership and agency. In fact, the coronavirus did for congregations what they could not do for themselves – get them moving!

As we face into the next crisis, we can choose to build on the strengths we have newly developed in the current crisis. We now know we are people who can adapt, if we choose to, even in the worst situations. There's no reason these newfound capacities can't be used well in the next good crisis before us. Remember how exhilarating it felt to adapt, pushing through our worry to discover something beautiful on the other side as we learned to grow, serve, meet, and worship in new ways. Let's continue to be resilient so we can see new ways of coming together across the miles. Let us distinguish between our identity as Christians and the institutions we have built and take ownership of the moment before us. The choice is ours.

Lift Up the Vision

Based on common and shared values, you can establish a vision for the community. Let your shared values extend out beyond you. It's not just you in the church who is prone to polarization; it's the community too. Communities long to be united, to feel safe, to thrive. Lift up a vision that draws people together. This vision is not a church improvement plan but, rather, a vision for what the community can become. I write about the five surprise elements of a Jesus-like dream in *Dream Like Jesus*. These elements include that the vision must expand assumptions about what is possible, be bigger than you, scare you, focus on the thriving of the community rather than the survival of the institution, and inspire and unify people.

We can't plan how to operate in an unknown future. But the more relaxed we are, the more we trust God, the more we'll be able to dance in the conversation with God and approach the unknown, knowing that we can survive and even thrive.

Focus on Your Neighborhood

John Wesley famously said, "The world is my parish." This belief allowed him to make a difference wherever he went, even as a circuit preacher who traveled all over, superintending and planting churches. The world is a bit different now. We can Zoom all over the world.

Ultimately, however, your greatest impact may be local.

For Rev. Alex Joyner, a Creating a Culture of Renewal® participant and pastor in Charlottesville, Virginia, the mission field is right across the street. That's where the 2017 "Unite the Right" rally ended with one person driving his car into a throng of people, killing one and injuring thirty-five others. Not only did the park feel tainted and off-limits by the hate enacted there, but it hung over the city as well. How can this community heal from such a tragedy? Alex's answer is his vision: "Love the whole city. Love the city whole. Starting right here." While deep wounds have plagued the community around the church he serves, he can now see and feel the church and community beginning to heal. The church has partnered with others to launch a 40-day prayer initiative in the park. Art initiatives, podcasts on the history and the future of Charlottesville, and a clean-up of the park are all underway as well.

As you live out the mission of the post-pandemic church, remember your mission field may be across cyberspace and also right across the street. The Kin(g)dom of God is both global and local. All the issues, joys, and concerns that might once have seemed "over there" are in your neighborhood. Sow into your community and keep it fertile by planting exactly where you are. Even as you open the doors of the hybrid church to people far and wide.

One Invitation Away from Returning

Now that your church is making these important culture shifts, it's time to let others know what you are offering! The common wisdom is that a church only has three weeks to connect with people who are absent. After that, they've internalized the message that you haven't missed them. With the pandemic, however, new rules apply. I believe that even people who left before the pandemic are one invitation away from returning. That's because the biggest reason people come back to church is that they are invited. One sincere, guilt-free invitation can make all the difference for those who simply got out of the habit during the pandemic or those looking for a life change.

These invitations can come in the form of a person-to-person invitation to a friend, relative, neighbor, or colleague. "Overall, 41% of the formerly churched said they would return to the local church if a friend or acquaintance invited them. Younger adults are even more influenced by the power of the invitation. Approximately 60% of those 18–35 would consider returning to church if someone they knew asked them to come back."[48]

If the biggest reason people come back to church is through an invitation, the biggest need driving people to church is because they feel an emptiness – something missing. Even though they may not be able to put it

FORGING A NEW PATH

into words, they need the very things you are offering. These include the need for God, community, belonging, a connection they can access online and offline, and a sense of awe and the miraculous in their life. You can help them fill that gap.

Sometimes an important life change gets a person thinking about God, spirituality, or eternity. This life change can be a birth, death, marriage, divorce, retirement, or some other dramatic change to their normal way of living. Perhaps they moved and are ready to find a church. They may come to church to connect with important truths to have guidance for their lives. Again, you can help them fill that gap.

After living virtually, people are eager to reconnect with humanity. When visitors come, go out of your way to greet and welcome them. Remember, people long to belong. They want to know they matter, and to be part of something larger than themselves.

Celebrate

As you grow the post-pandemic church, find people, places, and things to celebrate. Celebration is good for the soul. It's even a key component of healthy emotional intelligence. It draws communities together, builds bonds of happiness, and allows you to deepen your faith. It marks progress and gives you a chance to praise God. It reinforces the good you are doing.

Celebration is also biblical. Jesus used parables to demonstrate what we can celebrate. Celebrate when something lost is found, as in the parable of the lost sheep (Luke 15:3-7), the lost coin (Luke 15:8-10), or the parable of the prodigal son (Luke 15:11-32). In each story, when the shepherd found his sheep, when the woman found her coin, and when the father's son returned to him, they all "rejoiced." The takeaway of these three stories for us is don't take anything for granted – not one sheep, one coin, or especially one son. Rejoice over all that has been lost and now is found, like face-to-face worship and the simple joy of being together.

Then widen your focus from those in your church community to members of your larger community. Consider especially those who have been hardest hit by the pandemic. Mourn those you have lost, and celebrate those you have found, and give thanks for those who were there by your side all along. You might even consider how to have a celebration in the community for the community. For example, if someone completes probation, jail time, or prison time, celebrate them. When someone hits a milestone in recovery, celebrate them. When someone changes their circumstances in some way or renews their vows, consult "To Bless the Space Between Us," for ideas about what can be blessed that we might normally ignore or not have words for.

How you celebrate can take many forms. Here are some ways Jesus did it: hold dinner parties, prepare a festive meal, invite friends, and attend to the miracle in your midst. Or even rest and get away from it all. Taking a break from meetings is a form of celebration, too.

Celebrations are important mile markers that anchor memory and participation. Each of these forms of celebration also creates natural opportunities to invite and incorporate new people.

Of course, celebration is not limited to biblical examples. Celebration is a natural human expression of joy, thanksgiving, and contentment. Pick up on examples in your community by choosing a theme or a food that is endemic to your area. Since food is the foundation of community, consider a strawberry festival, a harvest festival, an Easter festival. Bring food to the endeavors. Also, feed people who don't have food. Drawing people together into community can be intimidating if you're working to have many people who don't know each other feel comfortable interacting with each other. Eating together can be one way to help people get to know one another if you create ways for them to interact while eating.

One reason we don't press forward into unknown futures is that we haven't paused to celebrate all that has gone well and right in the past. The biblical tithe was just that: a celebration of all the ways God had been present up until then. These tithes allowed people to go forward, continuing to trust God. It's time for that same ethos again.

When Pandemics End New Futures Begin

Pandemics end in one of three ways. Either the virus runs out of steam and operates at a low level of infection, or people simply grow tired of it and declare that it is over, or a brand-new innovation comes on the scene. All of these endings may be operative with COVID-19. Recently, The Atlantic magazine featured a story about how to wipe out not only the coronavirus but every respiratory virus at once. Before I tell you about that, though, let me give you a bit of history.

When London vanquished cholera in the nineteenth century, it wasn't a vaccine or a drug that resolved that health care crisis. It was a sewage system. The city's drinking water was intermingling with human waste, spreading bacteria in one deadly outbreak after another. Officials built a new comprehensive network of sewers that separated the two. London never experienced a major cholera outbreak after 1866. All that was needed was a re-engineering of the urban landscape.

In a similar way, yellow fever and malaria, which were rampant in the U.S. in the nineteenth and twentieth centuries, were not resolved through drugs or vaccines. Instead, those diseases were resolved through a combination of pesticides, wide-scale landscape management, and window screens that kept mosquitoes at bay. The resolution came not by focusing on the disease agent itself but on the environment in which it thrived: swampy lands. One by one, diseases that we had accepted as inevitable facts in life – dysentery, typhoid, and typhus, to name a few more – have been reduced or wiped out in the developing world. All of it has come by addressing the environments in which they develop and thrive.

Scientists and civil engineers have explored whether the COVID-19 pandemic could be resolved similarly. Instead of masks, vaccines, or even herd immunity, the solution may well lie in reimagining the air quality we breathe indoors. Scientists are now promoting the idea of re-imaging building ventilation in order to clean up indoor air.

Innovations such as these bypass the fights that polarize us – masks, vaccines, and the like – by changing the very environment in which pandemics thrive. The church has the same opportunity in front of it. Here's the thing: If nineteenth-century city planners can redesign sewage systems so that cholera goes away, and twentieth-century landscape planners can redesign landscapes and homes so yellow fever and malaria go away, and twenty-first-century civil engineers and scientists can redesign buildings so that the coronavirus and other respiratory viruses are resolved, then perhaps twenty-first-century congregations and their leaders, folks like you, can create life-giving environments in which polarization finds no foothold. But where spirituality and community, aided by the culture of technology, thrive. Where the flourishing of the Spirit transforms such that the social pandemics of our time come to an end. And new futures begin.

Yes, the world has changed. But so has the church. You have shrugged off the constraints of the past, risen to the occasion and navigated tremendous change. Now it's time to partner with God and bring new futures to life. Right in your own churches and neighborhoods. Together, in community, let us stay open to the inner prompting of the Holy Spirit as we journey into a beautiful, meaningful future with God.

Acknowledgments

Special thanks to Laura Bush, Jamie Snively, McKenzie Sefa, and the rest of my book-writing team, including Terrell L McTyer, Clayton Payne, Stephen Pudinski, and Charlotte Pridgen Randolph. Your audacious energy carried me through the project. I am thankful for our weekly sessions.

To my beautiful team of staff and faculty at Rebekah Simon-Peter Coaching and Consulting Inc., who continually forge a new path in bringing Creating a Culture of Renewal® to life; I am forever grateful. And special thanks to all the pastors, lay leaders, district superintendents, denominational executives, and faith-based entrepreneurs who, through Creating a Culture of Renewal®, are moving the church forward in a post-pandemic world. Your pioneering, energizing, affirming, inclusive, humble, deliberate, resolute, and commanding leadership has made all the difference throughout the pandemic. Your courage inspires me.

Finally, to Jesus, Jerry, and Joseph, and Dotty, your love and support mean everything.

Creating a Culture of Renewal®

If this book calls to you, I invite you to take your next step with us and join the Creating a Culture of Renewal® community.

CREATING A CULTURE OF RENEWAL®

Through three nine-month tracks, denominational leaders, clergy, and lay leaders are empowered to:

Craft a bold vision that exponentially expands what you and your congregation thought possible.

Dramatically increase the number of people actively engaged in ministry.

Transform a risk-averse culture into a congregation willing to *Dream Like Jesus*, enthusiastically tackling new initiatives and launching new ministries.

My team offers a wide range of workshops, programs, and coaching services for church leaders and congregations seeking renewal. For more information on the resources listed below, visit www. rebekahsimonpeter.com.

FREE RESOURCES:

Weekly thought-provoking blogs.

Weekly Leadership Mojo video series

DARE to *Dream Like Jesus* plan

Got Renewal? Assessment

WORKSHOPS:

Speed up the process of renewal while reducing resistance to change with monthly workshop offerings led by Rebekah and her team.

CONFERENCES AND EVENTS:

Rebekah is available to keynote on a wide variety of topics to engage and energize pastors, denominational leaders, and spiritual entrepreneurs. Visit *rebekahsimonpeter.com* to request her to speak at your event.

INDIVIDUAL COACHING:

Rebekah offers individual coaching for leaders ready to move beyond limited thinking and predictable results to transform their personal and professional lives.

For more information about these resources and services, visit *rebekahsimonpeter.com*.

Endnotes

1 The American Journal of Managed Care. "A Timeline of Covid-19 Developments in 2020." AJMC, January 1, 2021. https://www.ajmc.com/view/a-timeline-of-covid19-developments-in-2020.

2 Schor, Elana. "Are Church Services Considered 'Essential'? Depends Where You Live." Christianity Today. Associated Press, March 24, 2020. https://www.christianitytoday.com/news/2020/march/state-exemptions-church-covid-19-essential-services.html.

3 Adamy, Janet. "Churches Changed during the Pandemic and Many Aren't Going Back." The Wall Street Journal. Dow Jones & Company, November 12, 2021. https://www.wsj.com/articles/church-pandemic-covid-online-11636728162.

4 "Famine, the Black Death, and the Afterlife." Arts and Humanities Through the Eras. Encyclopedia.com. (March 1, 2022). https://www.encyclopedia.com/humanities/culture-magazines/famine-black-death-and-afterlife.

5 I discuss about us disciples becoming apostles or ambassadors of Jesus in *Dream Like Jesus* because I believe that's who Jesus wants his followers to become, both for our personal spiritual growth, and the growth of the Beloved Community.

6 Payne, Sarah. 2021. "As church attendance numbers fade across the nation and online services become very convenient..." December 29, 2021. https://www.facebook.com/sarah.b.payne.5.

7 Grant, Tobin. "The Great Decline: 60 years of religion in one graph." Religious News Service. Sociological Forum, January 27, 2014. https://religionnews.com/2014/01/27/great-decline-religion-united-states-one-graph/.

8 Banks, Adelle M. "New study examines how COVID has changed churches." The Christian Century, November 29, 2021. https://www.christiancentury.org/article/news/new-study-examines-how-covid-has-changed-churches.

9 Molla, Rani. "How Apple's iPhone changed the world: 10 years in 10 charts." Vox. Recode.com, June 26, 2017. https://www.vox.com/2017/6/26/15821652/iphone-apple-10-year-anniversary-launch-mobile-stats-smart-phone-steve-jobs.

10 Colarossi, Natalie. "How long it took to develop 12 other vaccines in history." Insider. Business Insider, July 18, 2020. https://www.businessinsider.com/how-long-it-took-to-develop-other-vaccines-in-history-2020-7#smallpox-1.

11 UN Women. "Women in science who are making a difference during the pandemic." UN Women. February 9, 2021.

12 Britannica, T. Editors of Encyclopaedia. "Black Death." Encyclopedia Britannica, August 27, 2021. https://www.britannica.com/event/Black-Death.

13 Roos, Dave. "How 5 of History's Worst Pandemics Finally Ended." History. March 17, 2020. https://www.history.com/news/pandemics-end-plague-cholera-black-death-smallpox.

14 Greenblatt, Stephen. "What Shakespeare actually wrote about the plague." The New Yorker. May 7, 2020. https://www.newyorker.com/culture/cultural-comment/what-shakespeare-actually-wrote-about-the-plague.

15 Nix, Elizabeth. "Did an apple really fall on Isaac Newton's head?" History. November 13, 2015. https://www.history.com/news/did-an-apple-really-fall-on-isaac-newtons-head.

16 Levenson, Thomas. "The truth about Isaac Newton's productive plague." The New Yorker. April 6, 2020. https://www.newyorker.com/culture/cultural-comment/the-truth-about-isaac-newtons-productive-plague.

17 Hdogar, "Black Death – Pandemic that Killed 200 Million People." Lessons in History. April 18, 2021. https://medium.com/lessons-from-history/black-death-pandemic-that-killed-200-million-people-7d94f2753465.

18 De Witte, Melissa. "For Renaissance Italians, combatting black plague was as much about politics as it was science, according to Stanford scholar." Stanford News Service. May 12, 2020. https://news.stanford.edu/2020/05/12/combating-black-plague-just-much-politics-science/.

19 Martin Luther. Luther's Works, Vol. 43: Devotional Writings II, ed. Jaroslav Jan Pelikan, Hilton C. Oswald, and Helmut T. Lehmann, vol. 43 (Philadelphia: Fortress Press, 1999), 119–38. https://www.christianitytoday.com/ct/2020/may-web-only/martin-luther-plague-pandemic-coronavirus-covid-flee-letter.html.

20 Roper, Lyndal. "When plague came to Wittenberg." London Review of Books. July 6, 2020. https://www.lrb.co.uk/blog/2020/july/when-plague-came-to-wittenberg. Whitaker, Robyn. "God, plagues and pestilence – what history can teach us about living through a pandemic." The Conversation. October 1, 2020. https://theconversation.com/god-plagues-and-pestilence-what-history-can-teach-us-about-living-through-a-pandemic-146094.

21 Zentner, McLaurine H., "The Black Death and Its Impact on the Church and Popular Religion" (2015). Honors Theses. 682. https://egrove.olemiss.edu/hon_thesis/682.

22 Cybulskie, Danièle. "Priests and the Black Death." Medievalists.net. April 16, 2022. https://www.medievalists.net/2015/02/priests-black-death/.

23 Mark, Joshua J.. "Religious Responses to the Black Death." World History Encyclopedia. Last modified April 16, 2020. https://www.worldhistory.org/article/1541/religious-responses-to-the-black-death/.

24 Wilkinson, Freddie. "The Protestant Reformation." National Geographic Society. April 7, 2021. https://www.nationalgeographic.org/article/protestant-reformation/.

25 Janis, Sharon, Spirituality for Dummies (Wiley & Sons, Incorporated, John, 2008).

26 https://www.trendhunter.com/report?ak=e2e069c7f9f85fbe523c04df701c28b5.

27 Jeanet Sinding Bentzen. "In crisis, we pray: Religiosity and the COVID-19 pandemic." Journal of Economic Behavior & Organization, Volume 192, 2021, Pages 541-583, ISSN 0167-2681, https://doi.org/10.1016/j.jebo.2021.10.014.

28 Livni, Ephrat. "Columbia and Yale scientists found the spiritual part of our brains – religion not required." Quartz. https://qz.com/1292368/columbia-and-yale-scientists-just-found-the-spiritual-part-of-our-brains/.

29 Fischer, Brad. "Spirituality Involves More than Just a 'God Spot' in the Brain." Sci Tech Daily. M News Bureau, April 20, 2012. https://scitechdaily.com/spirituality-involves-more-than-just-a-god-spot-in-the-brain/ 2012.

30 Norton, Amy. "Scientists Track Spirituality in the Human Brain." HealthDay Reporter. July 8, 2021. https://www.usnews.com/news/health-news/articles/2021-07-08/scientists-track-spirituality-in-the-human-brain.

31 Fowler, James. "Stages of Faith." Psychology Charts. 1981. http://psychologycharts.com/james-fowler-stages-of-faith.html.

32 Personal communication. January 16, 2022.

33 Leong, Ross, and Tickle. "Here comes the Great Resignation. Why millions of employees could quit their jobs post-pandemic." ABC News. This Working Life, September 23, 2021. https://www.abc.net.au/news/2021-09-24/the-great-resignation-post-pandemic-work-life-balance/100478866.

34 Elting, Liz. "The Incredibly Simple Reason Behind the Great Resignation." Forbes. November 11, 2021. https://www.forbes.com/sites/lizelting/2021/11/11/the-incredibly-simple-reason-behind-the-great-resignation/?sh=834d635c4b92.

35 Christian, Alex. "How the Great Resignation is turning into the Great Reshuffle." BBC Worklife. How We Work, December 14, 2021. https://www.bbc.com/worklife/article/20211214-great-resignation-into-great-reshuffle.

36 Floret-Bixler, Melissa. "Why Pastors are Joining the Great Resignation." Sojourners. November 30, 2021. https://sojo.net/articles/why-pastors-are-joining-great-resignation.

37 Trafton, Anne. "A hunger for social contact." Massachusetts Institute of Technology. MIT News, November 23, 2020. https://news.mit.edu/2020/hunger-social-cravings-neuroscience-1123.

38 Brower, Tracy. "Missing Your People: Why Belonging is so Important and How to Create It." Forbes. January 10, 2021. https://www.forbes.com/sites/tracybrower/2021/01/10/missing-your-people-why-belonging-is-so-important-and-how-to-create-it/?sh=29a2f1d67c43.

39 Buck and Hardwick. "A sense of belonging is what drives well-being – and it's disappearing." Fast Company. August 18, 2021. https://www.fastcompany.com/90666944/a-sense-of-belonging-is-what-drives-wellbeing-and-its-disappearing.

40 Farley, Todd. "Gen Z is made of zombies – less educated, more depressed, without values." New York Post. August 12, 2021. https://nypost.com/2021/08/21/gen-z-students-are-less-educated-more-depressed-and-lack-values/.

41 Ruth, Lizi. "Real Reasons Millenials Quit Church – written by a Millenial." Medium. August 12, 2021. https://medium.com/@Widowedat24/real-reasons-millenials-quit-church-written-by-a-millenial-b56a11a883dd.

42 Kubilus, Derek. "A Better Story: Addressing Conspiracy Theories with the Gospel." Faith + Lead Luther Seminary. February 9, 2022. https://faithlead.luthersem.edu/a-better-story-addressing-conspiracy-theories-with-the-gospel/?utm_medium=email&utm_source=sharpspring&sslid=Mze3sLA0tDQxtLA0AAA&sseid=MzK2tLSwMDYyMwMA&jobid=24c41966-36e9-4598-8562-88392fc75d34.

43 McKinsey and Company. "COVID-19: Implications for business." Executive Briefing. February 23, 2022. https://www.mckinsey.com/business-functions/risk-and-resilience/our-insights/covid-19-implications-for-business.

44 Roos, Dave. "7 Ways the Printing Press Changed the World." History. September 3, 2019. https://www.history.com/news/printing-press-renaissance.

45 Panzer, Ryan. "Digital ministry: More about culture than computers." Faith + Lead Luther Seminary. June 30, 2020. https://faithlead.luthersem.edu/digital-ministry-more-about-culture-than-computers/.

46 Personal communication. February 2021.

47 Will, Alex Shea. "Let's re-envision 'normal.'" Faith & Leadership. Duke University, April 20, 2021. https://faithandleadership.com/lets-re-envision-normal.

48 Rainer, Thom. "Why People Leave and How to Help Them Return to the Church." Church Leaders. January 14, 2022. https://churchleaders.com/outreach-missions/outreach-missions-articles/138855-coming-home-why-people-leave-the-church-and-how-to-bring-them-back.html.

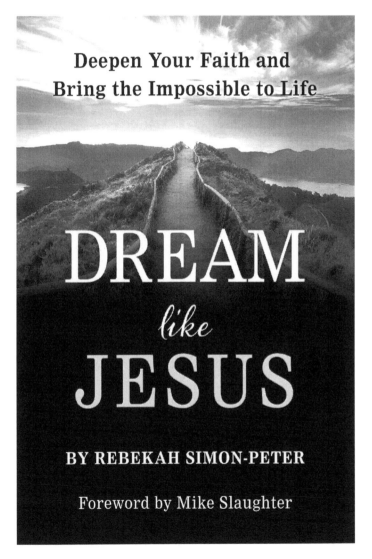

Other Books By
Rebekah Simon-Peter

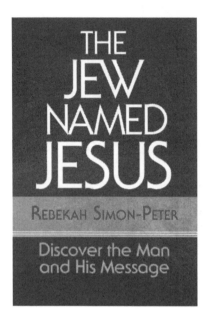

Other Books By
Market Square Publishing

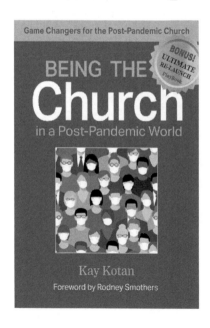

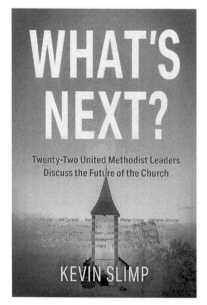

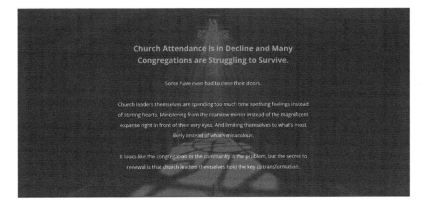

Made in the USA
Columbia, SC
05 May 2023

16143542R00100